LEAD THE FUTURE

LEAD THE FUTURE

STRATEGIES AND SYSTEMS
FOR EMERGING LEADERS

GRANT DEVER

NEW DEGREE PRESS

LEAD THE FUTURE

Strategies and Systems for Emerging Leaders

ISBN   978-1-64137-326-5   *Paperback*

            978-1-64137-632-7   *Ebook*

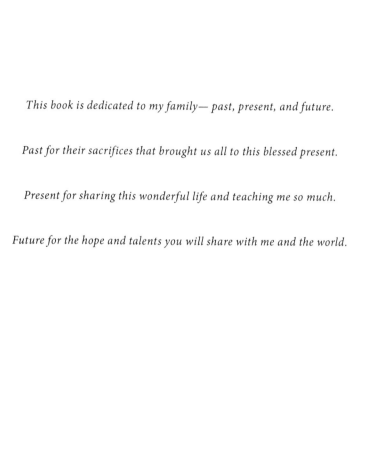

This book is dedicated to my family— past, present, and future.

Past for their sacrifices that brought us all to this blessed present.

Present for sharing this wonderful life and teaching me so much.

Future for the hope and talents you will share with me and the world.

CONTENTS

INTRODUCTION

WELCOME TO THE FELLOWSHIP

I do not know how you ended up reading or listening to this book, but it will change the way you view the world.

You likely already view yourself as a leader or at least aspire to be one. Or perhaps someone sees that potential within you. However you ended up here, you can still run away. It's not too late to donate this book to your local library. To leave the sword in the stone. To run from the ring before it sends you on an arduous, life-changing journey. To press pause on the audiobook, request a refund, and go back to binge-watching more episodes of *Hot Ones*.

Imagine the person you most admire, who has done something challenging, great, or consequential. This person may be a teacher, coach, parent, or a household name.

Now, ask yourself, *Why did they do it?*

I guarantee you no one forced them to rise to greatness. For every person who took action and persevered when things got tough, even more had the potential but lacked the drive or courage.

Most people's lives aren't like Frodo's. We can't all have a wizard push us out the door. Or have a magical giant rig the postal service to make sure we follow our destiny.

In other words, you can't rely on the universe to tap you on the shoulder and tell you the time has come to be awesome.

With this thought in mind, please consider your shoulder tapped.

BORN TO RUN

While no one walked up and literally tapped my shoulder, I am fortunate to have people in my life who encourage me to consider opportunities that have resulted in life-changing adventures.

"Grant, you should run to be the next president."

"No, you should, David."

"No. Seriously, you should actually run..."

My freshman-year roommate and then-outgoing vice president of our Students' Association Government at the University of Rochester, David Stark, encouraged me to run to be the next president. As you can see, my initial response wasn't enthusiastic. I wasn't sure if I was ready for the responsibility, or if that was how I wanted to spend my senior year at college. I had just finished my first semester of involvement with the student government, and it was a lot of work—hours and hours of meetings and emails every single week.

Later that night, I received a call from my brother Clark. We caught up after a few weeks of us both being busy.

"So, are you going to run to be the president of your school?"

"My freshman-year roommate David just tried to convince me that I should run. I'm not sure if I want to."

"You want people to view your university like it's Harvard, right?"

"Yeah."

"If you knew that you could be the student body president at Harvard, would I, or anyone, have to convince you to run?"

When Clark said that, I knew he was right. I had spent the last three years of my life serving my community in a variety of leadership roles, as president of my class council, a residential adviser, and as a mentor. I was sold on the idea that the University of Rochester would one day be further recognized as a world-class institution, and I knew I had a role to play in working toward that end. I had a few more conversations before I officially decided I was going to run a campaign, all the while talking myself into it.

Only two days before the deadline to declare our candidacy, I was able to convince my friend Melissa Holloway to run as my vice president. Melissa had been a great business manager for our class council, served as a senator in the student government, and been a leader in numerous service organizations. I knew that if I were going to take on such a demanding role, I needed a partner with her incredible work ethic, organizational skills, and competency.

The next day, our campaign began. We recruited friends to design posters and take campaign photos of us. We assembled a small team of people to help us poster and draft public endorsements for our campaign. We planned which student organizations to reach out to and what campus influencers to target for their support. We spent a couple hours in a Google Doc working to create our initial platform and spun up a campaign site using Wix.

When campaigning officially began, we were hardly ready to launch. We spent the next week talking with our peers, answering students' questions, and bombarding social media with campaign content. The entire process was stressful, but fun.

At one point, David checked in with me at Starbucks and said, "You guys aren't doing enough. If you don't step up your outreach, I'm pretty sure you're going to lose." I took his warning seriously, ordered another red-eye refill in my reusable mug, and spent the following three hours contacting almost everyone I had met in college asking for their support.

We participated in the debate, hosted by outgoing President Antoinette Esce. When it ended, we weren't sure how it had gone, but we were happy it was over. Earlier that day, we had met with the *Campus Times*, the student newspaper, for an interview. The next day, we were fortunate to receive their endorsement:

"Ultimately, after our interviews with the two pairs, we are confident in the Dever-Holloway ticket and their ability to represent the interests of the student body, building initiatives that are based on student desires, maintaining quality relationships with administrators and representing student interests," the *CT* wrote. "They are a friendly and personable team, qualities we believe will serve them well in the role of president and vice president, as well as benefit us, the students at the University of Rochester."[1]

Voting opened, and we continued to reach out to our friends to help rally the vote. All the Facebook likes and posts didn't mean anything if our friends wouldn't actually vote. The remaining hours of the campaign were spent in nervous anticipation. David's warning had resonated with me; I was worried that we would lose, and I had never lost a campaign race. When the polls closed, we were waiting with one of the *CT*'s photographers and editors in Starbucks. A different editor and photographer sat with our rivals.

We were refreshing the results page over and over. When the results finally came in, we found we had won with 71 percent of the total vote. Shocked, Melissa and I hugged each other, which made the front page of the next paper. At the time, we

---

1   (CT Staff 2019)

couldn't have known how this experience would challenge us, consume us, and change our lives forever.

Before my tenure as student body president, I thought that leadership was mainly about building and maintaining relationships, delegating tasks, and running productive meetings. The full-time immersion in servant leadership the role demanded opened my eyes to the breadth of activities involved in effective leadership, from hiring the right people, to managing a public brand, to knowing when to speak and when to listen.

Since completing my tenure as president, I have helped co-found, build, and launch a creative problem-solving space, program, and community at the University of Rochester called *iZone*. My responsibilities included hiring our team, developing our organizational model, managing our brand, and mentoring undergraduate entrepreneurs, problem-solvers, and creators.

My experience at iZone inspired me to write this book so I could share the insights that resonated with students and influenced many of our foundational decisions.

This book is a compilation of frameworks, stories, and perspectives that I hope will enable emerging leaders to accelerate their understanding of leadership and take action to solve problems and improve the lives of others.

Here are a few of the key topics we will explore in this book:

- Leadership as a mindset, not a hierarchy
- Ten principles all leaders should take to heart
- The existence of power laws and their influence on our world
- Why you need to figure out who your real friends are
- Thinking about your "skill stack" and creating your own luck

I firmly believe that exposure to new ideas can have a transformational impact on our lives. Different frameworks for thinking can give us insight when making decisions or trying to understand the world around us.

You'll hear stories including:

- How pessimism enabled greater access to drinking water throughout Africa
- How yelling, "WOOO!" at a conference made our event standing room only
- How learning German might be more valuable than getting a 4.0 GPA in law school
- How Kanye West can change your life
- How I started a mafia

While you have to develop mastery of the mindset and skill sets involved in leadership through experience, reading the insights and stories of others has also been critical to my success as a leader—and, in particular, reading the stories of those with wildly different experiences or who have solved problems I am experiencing in my own life. As I conducted my research for this book, I reread many texts that have greatly influenced my perspective and decision-making.

Milan Kundera writes in *The Unbearable Lightness of Being*, "Culture is perishing in overproduction, in an avalanche of words, in the madness of quantity."[2] In a world overflowing with content, people have to serve as curators and help surface and highlight the most potent and valuable ideas or works. Part of my goal in writing this book is also to save you time by sharing what I have learned from my mistakes, chasing ideas down rabbit holes, and obsessing over self-improvement. I aim to connect you to a breadth of condensed, perspective-altering ideas and their sources.

I love novelty and have spent countless hours reading nonfiction books, listening to podcasts, and asking questions of the smartest and most experienced people I know in order to learn something new. I am aware that many people begin to feel their eyes getting heavy even thinking about reading more than one nonfiction book (especially those of you listening to the audiobook). This book is also for you. I hope to share these tools with you in a short, relatively painless

---

2   ("A Quote From The Unbearable Lightness Of Being" 2019)

way and perhaps engage your curiosity and convince you to read my sources.

I wrote this book because I believe in each and every one of you.

I love humanity, and I know that we all have a role to play in mitigating suffering and leading our world toward a more prosperous and meaningful future. I know we all have a responsibility to positively impact the world. When I am at my worst—sleeping in, chronically online, and binge-consuming content—my avoidance of that responsibility drives my escapism. When I am at my best, that responsibility drives me to leap out of bed in the morning and strive to become a better version of myself.

Okay, one last chance. Do you want to turn back?

No?

Good. I didn't think so.

ACTION: Go grab a notebook and a pen. You will want them close by while reading (or listening) to this book. Not only will taking notes help you to remember the most powerful ideas but I have embedded more prompts like this throughout the book to encourage you to reflect and develop a plan for action. This book is not meant to be consumed and forgotten but rather to spur you to action and empower you to expand your leadership competencies.

My responses to many of these prompts will be available on www.grantdever.com.

CHAPTER 1

GRANTMAN ORIGINS

———

ORIGINS

I grew up in Honeoye Falls, a rural suburb of Rochester.

Honeoye Falls is a one-stoplight town with a population of 2,800. It is reminiscent of the ways rural American towns are portrayed in '80s movies like The Breakfast Club. Honeoye Falls is a warm community, where people know each other, attend the local sports games and parades, and support each other when tragedy strikes.

I grew up as a "second-generation child"—my phrase to describe the fact that my brother is ten years older than me. My parents divorced shortly after I was born. Their living in separate homes was normal to me. According to my mom, when I returned from my first sleepover, I was shocked that "Nick's mom and dad live in the same house!" My mom, dad, and stepmom have always been supportive of me and present throughout my life.

Being a second-generation child has been valuable because my brother Clark has been able to provide critical support and mentorship to me throughout my life. It also meant that my parents had already, unsuccessfully, tried to get one of their children involved in Cub Scouts and little league baseball. I was not forced to participate in many activities and grew up with a lot of autonomy.

I attended the local school district, Honeoye Falls–Lima. The Class of 2012 was the largest in recent history. We boasted a strong 208 students, which meant we knew most of each other's names and gossip went locally viral before the age of smartphones.

Of the 208 students in my graduating class, I was the youngest. My mom had a local babysitter and friendly grandmother, Mary Jo, watch and take care of me while she was at work. Students at Honeoye Falls commonly attended pre-K, but I did not. I was highly sociable, and my parents were already paying school taxes, so they decided to send me to kindergarten at age four.

Both my parents are college-educated and heavily value education. They expected that I would perform well in school and behave. However, compared to some of my friends' "helicopter parents," they were relatively hands-off. They were firm about their expectations and the boundaries I could not cross, but they didn't pressure me to be valedictorian or a star athlete.

In fact, growing up, I was one of the least athletic kids in my entire grade. I played little league soccer and eventually found a solid niche as goalie, partly because I was an incredibly slow runner. I was "pigeon-toed," and most other kids were more athletic than I was. In my small town, and I'm sure many others like it, you needed to be athletic to be considered cool. If you wanted to eat at the cool kids' table, you needed to be a gym class hero.

As early as third grade, we were mandated to run The Mile. In gym class, we would be notified that the next class we would be timed and assessed in our ability to run a course or complete four laps around the track. The night before The Mile, I was always unable to sleep, too distressed thinking about how I was about to embarrass myself. Until fifth grade, I would get all worked up and do crunches while in bed. My little kid brain hoped and thought that I might wake up with a six-pack and a seven-minute mile time. Needless to say, this strategy never worked.

Instead, my childhood was dominated by video games— mostly Pokemon, and later Neopets and Runescape. Clark accelerated my computer usage by giving me my first computer when I was eight years old. I experienced the internet for the first time then, using AOL Instant Messenger to communicate with Clark while he was studying at SUNY Buffalo. Clark created my first online username: grantman08.

I was not a cool kid. I was not always confident. I was not the kind of kid others would follow. But it didn't matter. I learned I could choose what kind of person I wanted to be, and grantman08 was about to choose to become a leader.

CHOOSING TO LEAD

My sixth-grade math teacher, Mrs. Gardner, started me on a path to greater self-confidence. She was the cross-country coach for the middle school team and tried to recruit all of us to join the team. When we were eligible to join school sports in seventh grade, I participated in cross-country running, cross-country skiing, and track.

At first, I was an awful athlete and had almost no discipline for training. I started every fall out of shape. I never overcame my lack of discipline and participated on these teams on and off until I quit organized sports during my junior year. However, going from running ten-minute miles in my seventh grade fall to 5:45-minute miles my sophomore spring did wonders for my self-esteem. I still wasn't cool, but I had close friends, good grades, and a positive self-image.

During the spring of my sophomore year, my friend group got the idea that we should all run for the class council. The junior class council had a role in designing and building the class float for our homecoming parade, in addition to helping plan prom. By the time my friends shared their idea with me, the only remaining role was secretary. I thought it sounded like fun, but I was not known for being particularly organized or taking notes. I usually had to ask my friends to remind me what our homework was.

At the time, my friend James Goodman was a senior and president of the executive student council. I told him about our idea and asked him for campaign advice. He told me I should run to be his successor as president of the executive student council instead and gave me some advice on how to run a campaign. In the end, I took his suggestion.

By my sophomore year, I was already a daily user of Facebook and utilized the platform to wage my campaign. I was competing against a junior girl, who was running with a group of her friends. My friends made posters and low-quality memes to support my campaign. I invited everyone I knew to like my campaign page, where we would share our posters. The image that most comes to mind is a picture of me lying on my desk, asleep in English class. One of my friends edited text onto it that said, "Vote Grant Dever, he'll put your problems to rest." My friends and I thought it was funny, and it got quite a bit of traction on Facebook.

Vote Grant Dever For Class Representative

"He'll put your problems to rest"

With my social media campaign and closer relationships with the freshmen, I won the election. I was surprised by the result, because it felt like I was an underdog, running alone against a group of upperclassmen. I was happy to have achieved my goal and excited for the opportunity. We were predominantly responsible for choosing the themes for our Spirit Week days and the homecoming floats, in addition to organizing the pep rally.

In our small-town school, Spirit Week and the pep rally were big events. Everyone would dress up for the various themes, and people went all-out to try to have the most enthusiastic costume. My favorite was "hipster day."

On Friday of Spirit Week, we had a home game and everyone wore our school colors—black and gold. The pep rally started at 1 p.m. and lasted until 3 p.m. when the buses arrived. The classes would be pitted against each other in various competitions: tug-of-war, relays, chanting competitions. We always left energized and ready to spend the night watching football.

While none of these responsibilities brought much stress to my life, taking on the identity of a leader changed my relationship with the world. I began to feel confident in my ability to make decisions and felt comfortable assuming more responsibility.

The following year, I convinced a few of my friends to run with me for my reelection campaign. I asked a sophomore with a lot of freshman friends, Nate Tiberio, to run as my vice president. We won that election, partially because people already saw me as the president. Not only did I have the incumbent's advantage, but I also projected my identity as the president. The changes were psychological, but they impacted my aspirations and behavior. This shift began to open my eyes to the importance of mindset and its relationship with leadership.

I became involved in other after school activities and felt passionate about my involvement in our community. I wasn't cool; I was a nerd—but I was popular. I had friends in all different cliques and class years. I spent most of my time doing the minimum amount of work to keep an A average, goofing around with my best friends, and playing an excessive amount of video games.

By the time I graduated high school, I was still poorly disciplined and lacked a lot of skills critical to leadership. I thought I was organized, professional, and capable of effectively leading groups. But mainly I knew how to use social media to win popularity contests, how to make a lot of different friends, and that I could rise to the occasion if I challenged myself.

I had no concept of how much more challenging leadership could become and how those experiences would accelerate my personal growth.

CHAPTER 2

DEFINING LEADERSHIP

DEFINING LEADERSHIP

What is in a name? That which we call a leader by any other name would influence as well.

—WILLIAM SHAKESPEARE (KIND OF)

This book is in part about the power of effective communication. A key part of effective communication is ensuring that members of the conversation agree on the meaning behind the word or concept they're discussing. Otherwise, you run the risk of everyone talking about different concepts and talking past one another. For example, telling a classroom of children they have to respect the teacher is not sufficient. They need to know what respect means and how to act it out.

So, for us to discuss leadership, we must agree on a definition. If you asked people on the street, "What is leadership?" they would have different images in their heads as they tried to describe it.

One person's response might focus on hierarchy, power, and authority: "My boss is the leader of our organization. He makes sure we show up to work and finish our tasks on time. If I screw up, he's the one who is going to let me know." All of these qualities are associated with leadership but not necessary for one to be a leader.

Another person may hear the word leader and imagine President Abraham Lincoln, with his dark brown beard standing in front of an audience, wearing a black suit with a black tie, a pocket watch ticking against his ribs, his iconic black top hat towering over everyone around him. His voice leads the crowd before him: "...and this nation, under God, shall have a new birth of freedom..." However, when we think of Lincoln, it's not the title of "president" that makes us perceive him as a leader but rather his vision, actions, and impact.

We might experience leadership when an elderly man suddenly collapses in a public park and everyone stops and stares. In the next moment, a woman rushes to assist him. She looks back at the crowd, points at a young man wearing crimson chinos and a plain white tee and says, "You call for help!"

She then points at a group of people nearby. "Do any of you know CPR?" she asks, and a young woman with curly brown hair responds, "Yes, I'm a lifeguard," and rushes over to help.

This woman did not have a role in a discrete hierarchy but was certainly the leader needed to handle the situation.

We also associate management with leadership.

Managers light a fire under people; leaders light a fire in people.
—KATHY AUSTIN, AUTHOR[3]

To separate leadership from management in our heads, let's use a sports analogy.

In middle-school soccer, the coach is evidently at the very least a manager. He ensures that everyone on the team is on time, wearing the appropriate gear, and not doing anything forbidden that would hurt the team's chance at victory, like cursing at the referee. The coach is there to maintain order but may not be the person who lights a fire within the team members. The true leader of the team might be their seventh-grade goalie, Henry. He doesn't hold any formal position in the hierarchy.

---

3   (Austin 2019)

Henry takes the time to provide positive feedback when one of his teammates has clearly been practicing on the weekends. Henry practices his drills for at least twenty minutes every day. Henry shows up to the preseason practices with greater speed and dexterity than he had at the peak of last season. Henry takes the time to reach out to sixth-grade students and give them feedback, like "Don't worry about Johnny—he's all talk," or "You should be sure to drill on your handling; you do the same move every time." The coach could be both a leader and a manager. Henry, however, is a leader but not a manager.

If being above others in a hierarchy, wielding power and authority, and fulfilling the tasks of management are not sufficient for one to be a leader, what does being a leader mean?

THINK: Take a minute to brainstorm a list of six people who come to mind when you hear the word "leader."

Every great dream begins with a dreamer. Always remember, you have within you the strength, the patience, and the passion to reach for the stars to change the world.

—HARRIET TUBMAN, AMERICAN ABOLITIONIST

AND CIVIL RIGHTS LEADER[4]

---

4   ("A Quote By Harriet Tubman" 2019)

Leadership is lifting a person's vision to high sights, the raising of a person's performance to a higher standard, the building of a personality beyond its normal limitations.

—PETER DRUCKER, MANAGEMENT CONSULTANT,

MBA PROFESSOR, AND BEST-SELLING AUTHOR[5]

A genuine leader is not a searcher for consensus but a molder of consensus.

—MARTIN LUTHER KING JR., BAPTIST

MINISTER AND CIVIL RIGHTS LEADER[6]

Reflecting on the quotes above, you probably know people who exemplify these qualities. Do any of these resonate with the people you wrote in your list? Do you perhaps see these qualities in yourself?

As we discussed earlier, you don't need to be the CEO of a major corporation or the prime minister of a country to be a leader. In fact, you might not need to have any real relationship with the people you're leading at all. Remember the woman who exercised her leadership to help the collapsed stranger?

---

5   ("A Quote From Management" 2019)
6   ("Martin Luther King, Jr. Quotes" 2019)

The definition of leader we will use throughout this book is: *any individual who takes any explicit action to influence others and align reality with their vision for the future.*

This definition encompasses something as simple as envisioning a clean sidewalk and convincing your neighbors to join you in taking twenty minutes to pick up the trash on your street, or as complex as winning popular support and raising funds to create a monorail that runs through your city of 206,000 people.

In February 2019, I visited California for the first time in my life. I attended AshokaU Exchange 2019—"a home for creative problem solvers, learners, listeners, and visionaries"—in beautiful, sunny San Diego.[7] I went as part of my job and got to share the experience with members of my team. Everyone from our team was participating in the conference: moderating a panel discussion, hosting a meet-up, or presenting. One of our employees, Deniz Cengiz, was hosting a rendition of one of our regular events at iZone, Screw Up Night.

The conference began as most do, with a buffet of carbs and coffee and a keynote address. As I entered the conference room, I heard the speaker inviting all the members to various

---

7   ("Ashoka U Exchange 2019: Beyond Boundaries & Borders - The Association For The Advancement Of Sustainability In Higher Education" 2019)

special programs throughout the day. She continued on to mention, "The Barbara J. Burger iZone from the University of Rochester will be hosting 'Ashoka Afterdark: Screw Up Night,' where everyone can share their failures and laugh about them." As I stood there for what seemed like seconds, but probably wasn't, I waited for applause to begin. I then shouted, "WOOO!" and began clapping as loud as I could, and the crowd erupted in applause.

Screw Up Night was a total success. By the time the event started, only standing room was available, and we had more volunteers to share stories than we had time for them to speak. The stories were excellent, and the room was filled with laughter and positive vibes. We can't know that it wouldn't have been as full had I not yelled, "WOOO!" but I assume that my actions had an impact.

This example is now my favorite to demonstrate what I mean by leadership: *taking any explicit action in order to influence others and align reality with your vision for the future.*

When you stop to consider the anecdote above, it becomes quite clear that anyone can become a leader, or at least choose to identify and act as one in a specific context.

What do Harriet Tubman, Peter Drucker, Abraham Lincoln, and I share? Clearly not level of impact or name recognition, but rather a desire and ability to turn our dreams, even the little ones, into realities.

We all recognize that formal hierarchy, authority, or power are not requisite to act as a leader. We feel that we can have a positive impact on the world and are willing to accept the responsibility that comes with the decision to act. Imagine yourself standing alongside any of us, or the person who you pictured in your mind when you read the quotes above. Doing so is the simple first step toward seeing yourself as a leader.

REFLECT: Take a minute to write down your own thoughts on leadership. If you don't know how to start, just write "I want to be a leader" until you get so bored that you choose to write something more interesting. Seriously, do it.

CHAPTER 3

PRINCIPLES OF LEADERSHIP

PRINCIPLES OF LEADERSHIP

Last year, I was selected by the Greater Rochester Chamber of Commerce to participate in its professional development program, CLIMB (Chamber Leadership Initiative: Mentoring For Business). All participants were required to read *The Truth About Leadership* by best-selling authors James M. Kouzes and Barry Z. Posner. While I had spent years of introspection on this topic, I found their research and clarification of the principles of leadership quite insightful.

We will use their research as a jumping-off point to discuss principles related to leadership. We will further explore these themes throughout the book, and I will note the related chapter(s). If a particular theme seems relevant or insightful, please consider flipping the pages in the book and pursuing that interest.

Just because books have a first page and a last page doesn't mean you need to read them in order.

1. "YOU MAKE A DIFFERENCE."

This statement is the first truth from Kouzes and Posner's research.[8] I hope all of you already believe that your actions make a difference. At the very least, please know that I believe your actions will make a difference. If I didn't, I would not have spent months of my life writing this book. We have many problems to solve, and I'm convinced that you're part of the solution.

Beyond the direct impact of your actions, you need to accept that you're a role model for others. Being a role model is not something you get to choose; you only get to decide if you'll be a positive or a negative one.

A common assumption suggests that the biggest role models, especially for young people, are all famous:

---

8   (Kouzes and Posner 2010)

- Business titans like Elon Musk or Ray Dalio
- Music superstars like Kanye West or Taylor Swift
- Professional athletes like Megan Rapinoe or Lebron James

However, according to Kouzes and Posner's research, that supposition is far from the truth.

For respondents eighteen to thirty years old, these were the results of their research[9]:

- Family member (40%)
- Teacher or coach (26%)
- Community or religious leader (11%)
- Business leader (7%)
- Professional athlete or entertainer (5%)
- Other (11%)

With this knowledge comes even more responsibility. If you aren't someone's role model now, you will be one day. I warned you in the introduction. As a leader, you need to accept that every action you take has consequences.

CONSIDER: Write down a list of what you see as the three most important qualities a leader should have. Why did you choose these three? Can you think of an example of a leader,

---

9   (Kouzes and Posner 2010)

in your life or otherwise, who demonstrates these qualities especially well? Can you think of anyone who is considered a leader but does not demonstrate these qualities?

2. "CREDIBILITY IS THE FOUNDATION OF LEADERSHIP."

A credible leader is someone who can demonstrate both competence and trustworthiness. They have a strength of character that encourages others to respect them. As someone choosing to identify as a leader, you need to prioritize building credibility. To convince anyone to follow you, you're going to have to demonstrate that you're someone worth following.

Kouzes and Posner have conducted extensive research on the topic of credibility in leadership. In a survey that included people from Africa, North America, South America, Asia, Europe, and Australia, respondents were asked to select out of twenty options seven characteristics they felt were required for a leader to be admirable.

Four qualities stood out as being the most important:

- Honest (85%)
- Forward-looking (70%)
- Inspiring (69%)
- Competent (64%)

The next-highest selected quality was "intelligent" with 42 percent of respondents, a sharp decrease from the others.[10]

Kouzes and Posner's research also suggests that the credibility of a leader has a significant impact on the behavior of other members in the organization.

For example, they found that when people perceived their manager as highly credible, their pride, sense of ownership within the organization, and intrinsic motivation to do their best were much stronger.

In contrast, when people perceived their manager as noncredible, their motivations to perform were solely extrinsic, and they demonstrated an overall sense of pessimism surrounding their organization.[11]

If you have ever had a great manager, you know how that can completely change how you feel about your work. I was fortunate that my boss at iZone, Julia Maddox, demonstrated a high degree of credibility. She made it clear from the beginning that she valued honesty and was always direct about any problems she noticed. Furthermore, whenever someone on our team made a mistake, she responded by calmly accepting

---

10   (Kouzes and Posner 2010)
11   (Kouzes and Posner 2010)

the reality of the situation and committing her expertise to help remedy it. Her leadership trickled down throughout the organization and drove our entire team to feel engaged in our work. We followed her example and worked hard to realize her vision. Likewise, if you have ever been a part of an organization in decline or stasis, you likely felt the impact of low credibility in the room every time the "leader" of the organization walked through.

As you work to develop your credibility, focus on being:

- Honest
- Forward-looking
- Inspiring
- Competent

REFLECT: Take some time to write about concrete actions you can take to improve your perception as someone who is honest, forward-looking, inspiring, and competent. Consider: Which of these might you need to work on the most? Which of these do you consider strengths? How might you create a system to develop these qualities over time?

3. "VALUES DRIVE COMMITMENT."

The people working with you want to know why you get out of bed every morning. They want to know what you're willing to fight for. They want to know about your past and what you're about.

Yes, you—not the organization. They want to know what you really believe, not just what's posted on the company's "about" page. You must have answers to these questions and authentically act out your values.[12]

John Mackey, co-founder of Whole Foods, established himself as the go-to example of an authentic, values-driven CEO: "My most important mission has always been to improve people's health and longevity through selling natural and organic whole foods and that is why I co-founded Whole Foods Market 40 years ago. I believe Whole Foods has been very successful in helping to evolve our food system in many positive and healthy ways."[13]

This statement was not just part of a PR campaign. Throughout Mackey's career, he has sparked a lot of criticism by being unabashed in his belief about the relationship between the quality of the food we consume and societal problems, as well as his commitment to capitalism. In particular, he generated significant backlash when he published an op-ed in the *Wall Street Journal* titled "The Whole Foods Alternative

---

12   (Kouzes and Posner 2010)
13   (Schumacher 2019)

to Obamacare," in which he made several policy recommendations and stated his beliefs about the need to improve America's diet.[14]

"He's so who he is every minute of every day," noted Glenda Flanagan, former CFO of Whole Foods, who served there for twenty-nine years. "He doesn't change who he is for anybody or any circumstance."[15]

His employees know he is genuine in his beliefs and, even if they disagree on particular issues, they respect his authenticity and commitment to the Whole Foods mission.

Kouzes and Posner write that while a CEO and their organization should have clearly articulated, shared values, even more critically, individuals who make up that organization should have clear personal values.

In their research, they assessed how committed individuals were to their organizations, based on their clarity about their own personal values and the values of the organization. For simplicity, they broke down their findings into a four-quadrant model:

---

14 (Mackey 2009)
15 (Kowitt 2015)

High-clarity of Personal Values, Low-clarity of Organizational Values	High-clarity of Personal Values, High-clarity of Organizational Values
6.12	6.26
Low-clarity of Personal Values, Low-clarity of Organizational Values	Low-clarity of Personal Values, High-clarity of Organizational Values
4.90	4.87

Their research found that high clarity of personal values is more important to an individual's commitment to their work than a high clarity of organizational values. The research showed no statistically significant difference between the commitment of workers who had low clarity of organizational values versus high clarity, unless they were accompanied by a high clarity of personal values.[16]

My friend Emma Pollock, who served in my executive cabinet and now works at IBM as a senior consultant focused on automation in government, verified this insight:

> I am a mission-driven individual and I need a reason to get out of bed every morning. Coming into work with an understanding of the mission of the organization and the importance of my contributions excites me. I have always felt compelled to service and knowing that my work is directly improving

---

16   (Kouzes and Posner 2010)

people's lives keeps me motivated and passionate about expanding my competency.

Even back in college, the tangible impact I had on our community—from improving the bus services to expanding options in the dining hall—made all of the time I spent worth it... I just want to make my communities and the world better for everyone.

If you want to build a committed team, you need to spend significant time thinking about values—your organization's as well as your own. Ideally, through that process, you will empower your collaborators to discover their individual values as well.

WRITE: *As we just learned, all employees, especially leaders, must know their own personal values. Take some time to consider what your top five values are and write about why.*

4. "FOCUSING ON THE FUTURE SETS LEADERS APART."

Since you are reading a book called *Lead the Future*, I am confident you are interested in the future and understand the importance of taking time to think about it. We will explore tactics for working to know yourself and thinking about the future in chapter nine, "80/20 Habits of Highly Effective Leaders."

This struggle is critical for all leaders. Once you are in a decision-making role, you will find more demands for your attention than minutes in the day. The only way to maintain a focus on the future is to commit explicit time in your schedule to think deeply about it.[17]

As one of the co-founders of iZone, I needed to consider external trends and think about the long-run impacts of our decisions. However, we also needed to focus most of our limited resources on the execution of our pilot programs and events. If we failed to create a strong first impression with students at the University of Rochester, we would struggle to build credibility, excitement, and engagement.

To build a better understanding of the future, I focused a significant portion of my time outside of work to expand my understanding of organizational design and trends in employment, higher education, and entrepreneurship.

I was able to make time to think proactively by:

---

17   (Kouzes and Posner 2010)

- Listening to audiobooks and podcasts focused on technology and business while commuting, eating, and exercising

- Blocking off two hours throughout my week to reflect—pen to paper—on our work and prioritize the problems we had identified

- Taking the time to seek feedback from our employees and paying special attention to how we could improve their experience

- Scheduling time for me and my boss to review feedback, evaluate our metrics, and prioritize opportunities

In particular, focusing on our employees and figuring out how to better engage them was the most important way to better prepare for the future. Our employees make up the bulk of our weekly labor hours and created most of our best events and programs. For our organization to thrive in the long run, we needed to focus on retaining our team members and creating an experience that would make others excited to work for us. We will explore this more in chapter six "iZone Mafia."

5. "YOU CAN'T DO IT ALONE."

Two of the themes we will continue to contemplate throughout the book are the complexity of our world and the importance of your collaborators. Obtaining true mastery over even a small part of any field is difficult and can take a lifetime. To solve challenging problems, you have to build partnerships and collaborate.[18]

People are extremely varied in their talents—you probably know people who are skilled athletes, talented artists, and hilarious comedians. But if you know one person who has all three of those attributes, I would also bet that they are not the greatest athlete, the most talented artist, or the most hilarious comedian.

For a clear example, consider a skill like visual design. At iZone, we needed to generate an endless stream of visual content to promote our events, differentiate our brand, and expand our reach on social media.

When we first started, the director, Julia, created most of our posters and graphics. If we gave her enough time, she could create a fine poster that we could use for our promotions. But as director, Julia had several other responsibilities—she was a capable designer, but that was not her specialty.

Our decision to hire Michael Keane as a dedicated visual designer was a game-changer. Not only was his visual content

---

18   (Kouzes and Posner 2010)

more engaging (sorry, Julia), but he was able to generate content much quicker. Perhaps most importantly, hiring Michael freed Julia up to leverage her skills where they could be most valuable to our organization and, as the director, she needed every minute she could find.

This insight is critical to your long-term success as a leader. The challenges that are engaging enough to motivate you to get out of bed every morning will require you to work with others. To solve complex problems, accept that you will need to find co-conspirators who will contribute their specific skill sets to help you on your mission. So keep your eyes open when meeting new people, because someday they might be just the collaborator your project needs.

6. "TRUST RULES."

According to Gallup's 2019 Confidence in [American] Institutions survey, of the seventeen institutions inquired about, only three received above 50 percent in "great deal/quite a lot" of confidence: small business, the police, and the military. Most institutions received a score of below 30 percent, and many ranked even lower than that. Notably, public schools received 29 percent, newspapers received 23 percent, news on the internet received 16 percent, and Congress received 11 percent.[19]

---

19 (Gallup 2019)

At a time when trust in our institutions is at such a low, trustworthy leaders could not be more valuable. Our leaders must understand how to build trust and what mistakes to avoid to prevent its deterioration. Trust is earned by taking responsibility and keeping your promises. It is destroyed by your actions or words conflicting with others' expectations of you.

Furthermore, an asymmetry exists between the rate at which you can create and destroy trust. One example of dishonesty or failed follow-through erodes more trust than one instance where you kept your word or did what you said you would builds it.

In *The Truth About Leadership*, Kouzes and Posner share the story of Gail McGovern, the president and CEO of the American Red Cross: "Gail was touring the nation and introducing herself to the organization's regional leaders and this trust question was put to her point-blank in one of those meetings: 'Can we trust you?' Gail's response was 'I can't answer that for you, but let me tell you that I trust each and every one of you.'"[20]

Gail understood that to earn the trust of her subordinates, she needed to trust them first. Of course, not everyone is worthy of your trust but, in most work environments, you

---

20 (Kouzes and Posner 2010)

should ideally start with the assumption that they are. You don't need to invite everyone over to your house, but you should start by trusting them to do their jobs competently and honestly.

To build the trust of your team and partners, you will need the strength to be vulnerable. To maintain the trust of your team and partners, you will need the diligence to keep your word. In the pursuit of building trust, you will bolster your credibility through honest speech and competent follow-through.

7. "LEADERSHIP IS AN AFFAIR OF THE HEART."

If you want your collaborators to give you not only their time but also their attention, energy, and creativity, you need to demonstrate that you genuinely care about them and are grateful for their contributions. To do so, you will have to be open, thoughtful, and authentic in your interactions with others. Similar to building trust, you need to lead with positivity and gratitude if you want others to reciprocate.

Research indicates that the highest-performing managers and leaders are the most open and caring. The best leaders demonstrate more affection toward others and want others to be more open with them. They are more positive and passionate, more loving and compassionate, and more grateful and encouraging than their lower performing counterparts.[21]

My friend Julianne McAdams' experience is not an uncommon one: "I once interned for a company whose mission was awesome and my coworkers were a lot of fun, but the boss was super condescending," she recalled. "I think it was because he was so passionate about the company, it was his baby, but he felt that this meant his ideas were superior to his employees'. He'd speak about projections and strategies and the works, and you could feel people rolling their eyes. I and my co-interns didn't miss that atmosphere when we were gone."

If you want people to love their work, you need to create the type of environment that makes them excited to show up and contribute every day. This atmosphere is important at any level of management within an organization, and particularly when you're working with volunteers. A common truism in business is that "employees leave managers, not companies," and Gallup research validated this claim: "50% of employees have left a job to get away from a manager at some point in their career."[22]

---

21 (Kouzes and Posner 2010)
22 (Gallup 2019)

While everything else in this chapter has been critical, you must especially recognize that your success as a leader will be limited if people do not like you. They may love the mission and their day-to-day job and even respect you, but they won't want to stick around if their manager makes them miserable.

8. "CHALLENGE IS THE CRUCIBLE FOR GREATNESS."

Our world faces massive, complex challenges: global poverty, environmental disaster, tensions between countries with incomprehensible military capabilities, and unfortunately the list goes on. As leaders, we need to each determine which challenge(s) we should dedicate our attention and energy to solving.

Like we considered earlier—to solve these problems, we will need to empower others and identify critical collaborators. No one can solve these challenges alone, and we cannot wait for others to solve them. We all have a role to play in helping humanity to confront these challenges.

Everything around you that you call "life" was made up by people who were no smarter than you. And you can change it, you can influence it, you can build your own things that other people can use.

—STEVE JOBS, CO-FOUNDER AND CEO
OF APPLE, CHAIRMAN OF PIXAR

If we take on challenges that are too difficult, we may end up overwhelmed and ineffective. If we take on challenges that are too easy, we will reduce our positive impact and miss out on opportunities to improve our skills. We should seek out "Goldilocks challenges"—ones that push us hard enough to help us grow and enable us to create a positive impact without breaking our spirits.

We will explore different frameworks for thinking about challenges and making decisions in chapters five and eight.

9. "YOU EITHER LEAD BY EXAMPLE OR YOU DON'T LEAD AT ALL."

This statement is an extension of "Credibility Is the Foundation of Leadership." If you play the game of "do as I say, not as I do," you cannot be a leader. As we discussed above, 85 percent of respondents identified honesty as a necessary quality in an admirable leader. Leading by example is honesty in action.

The respondents again emphasized this point to Kouzes and Posner. When asked, "What is credibility behaviorally? How do you know it when you see it?" the most frequent response they received was "You have to do what you say you will do."[23]

---

23 (Kouzes and Posner 2010)

If you are unable to live up to your word, in most cases the next best option is to be radically honest about your inability to. Take responsibility for your mistake. A person who promises, doesn't deliver, but apologizes made a mistake. A person who promises, doesn't deliver, and doesn't admit they made a mistake is a liar.

In chapter eight, we will carefully consider the importance of keeping your word and viewing the world through a positive-sum lens.

10. "THE BEST LEADERS ARE THE BEST LEARNERS."

Leadership is complex. Even in its most condensed form, we've broken it down into ten different principles. The terrible part is that there's more to learn than you can ever learn. The great part is that, as mentioned earlier, trying to learn everything is unnecessary because we can collaborate with others who have different knowledge and strengths. We can all continue to strive to improve our competency, and we all have a lifetime to hone our skills through work and service.

The important point is that leadership can be learned and that consistent attention to feedback is critical to improvement.

In *The Truth About Leadership*, Kouzes and Posner reference research by Bob Eichinger, Mike Lombardo, and Dave Ulrich:

"The single best predictor of future success in new and different managerial jobs is learning agility. 'Learning agility,' as they define it, 'is the ability to reflect on experience and then engage in new behaviors based on those reflections.'"[24]

You can't get around the truth: if you want to excel at anything, you need deliberate practice.

As you continue your development as a leader, you have to reflect on your strengths and the times in your life when you performed at your highest level. You must aspire toward mastery in some field, game, or skill, because it will give you insight into the discipline required to truly excel at anything. Until you experience the depth involved in performing at a high level, you cannot truly understand it.

My first experience performing at a high level wasn't in leadership, academics, music, or even athletics. I learned about the distinction between high-level and elite performance, commonly referred to as the "skill cap," through my experience playing *Call of Duty: World at War* on Xbox Live. I made friends with a team of elite players, and we were able to win over 300 games of Headquarters in a row, often by extreme margins.

---

24 (Kouzes and Posner 2010)

REFLECT: In which domain have you performed at your highest level? What did you understand that people at a lower skill didn't? How significant was the gap between you and the world's best performers?

Whatever experience you have with high-level performance, extrapolate that understanding to various skills that you want to develop throughout your life. If you want to truly excel, you will need to put in a lot of effort and work hard to expand your technique and understanding of the field. You will need to not only refine what you know, but also consciously identify what you don't know and where your weaknesses are. In chapter seven, we will discuss "skill stacks" and a framework for thinking about work in the face of our uncertain future.

Now that we've established our definition and surveyed the basic principles of leadership, we can dive into more actionable frameworks and models.

To review, these are the ten truths we explored in this chapter:

- You Make a Difference.
- Credibility Is the Foundation of Leadership.
- Values Drive Commitment.
- Focusing on the Future Sets Leaders Apart.
- You Can't Do It Alone.

- Trust Rules.
- Leadership Is an Affair of the Heart.
- Challenge Is the Crucible for Greatness.
- You Either Lead by Example or You Don't Lead at All.
- The Best Leaders Are the Best Learners.

Writing this chapter and working through the exercises helped me refine my understanding of these principles and reflect on how they resonate with my experience. Be sure to take the time to go through the exercises suggested throughout the chapter or use another method to reflect on the material. The more attention and energy you spend internalizing these principles and acting them out, the more powerful an effect they will have on your leadership practice.

ACTION: Write out each of these principles in your own words. Consider adding The Truth About Leadership *by Kouzes and Posner to your to-read list.*

CHAPTER 4

REALITIES OF LEADERSHIP

———

I wanted to do a great job as student body president. My predecessor, Antoinette Esce, now Antoinette Esce, M.D., was one of the highest-performing presidents in university history. She is a brilliant leader with a powerful imagination and incredible work ethic.

Knowing that I had big shoes to fill, I tried to prepare my mind and body for the year ahead. I solicited requests for leadership book recommendations, gave up my coffee addiction, ate healthy, meditated daily, reached out to prior presidents from the University of Rochester and other schools for advice, worked out at least three days a week, and strove to sleep eight hours every night. I felt incredible. My mind was well-organized, my body was strong, and although I was anxious for the year ahead, I felt excited and ready to face any challenge.

By the time the school year started, I was in the best shape of my life. On the day of Convocation, when the student body president addresses the incoming class, I didn't even need coffee to wake up. I wore a navy suit with a gold tie. My long flowing mane was wavy and informed the crowd that my real aspiration was to be a rock star. And I felt like one, too, as I looked out into the crowd of 2,000 people: the incoming class, their parents, and the university administration. They were smiling back at me as I began to address them.

The speech went perfectly. It was simple, people laughed at my jokes, and the energy was excellent. If the rest of the school year was going to be this good, I was ready to crush it. I would work hard, wake up early, be an excellent president and a great friend, bring up my GPA, and continue to live my disciplined life. After the speech, everyone I knew walked up to me, told me I did a great job, and gave me a hug or a high-five.

I was on top of the world.

REALITY STRIKES BACK

Everyone has a plan until they get punched in the mouth.

—MIKE TYSON[25]

In reality, I do think I was a great president in many ways. I'm proud of my team, our collaborators, and all that our administration was able to accomplish.

Here are a few of the results of all our work:

- The successful implementation of a new set of bylaws and organizational structure, ratified by the previous administration

---

25 ("Mike Tyson Quotes" 2019)

- Increased access to all-gender restroom options, resulting in the creation of over twenty bathrooms or renovations

- The abolition of stipends for student government leadership and the reallocation of those funds toward an annual $6,000 Community Building Fund—we threw the first Student Government Formal with the small portion of the funds we were able to access at the end of the year

- Changes to the College's communications strategies and policies for various incidents related to negative student experiences: severe winter storms, dorm flooding resulting in the damage of students' personal possessions, etc.

- Public letter in collaboration with other local colleges and universities to urge New York state legislators to permit operation of ride-sharing services in Rochester

- Various improvements to student services such as dining, transportation, accessibility, and other accommodations

However, the rest of it? That's not how it played out at all.

I was an okay friend. I prioritized my service, and a lot of dumb things, over my friendships, which has impacted my life in innumerable ways. My GPA was damaged as I did not leave enough space to excel in any of my courses. I only worked out once the entire year. I became addicted to coffee and would drink two thermoses of Starbucks Veranda blend every day. I ate a ton of greasy, low-quality food, and y'know the "Freshman 15"? I put on the Presidential 20. I would stay up late finishing my assignments the day before they were due and arrive home after 1 a.m. every night. I would wake up with just enough time to shower, grab coffee, and attend my first meeting of the day. I would be lying if I said I was never late.

As I mentioned earlier, I knew this role would be difficult and I would need good habits to thrive. The issue was that I was woefully unprepared for the accelerating stress of the role. The daily bombardment of requests, work, and decisions wore me down and sent me into a spiral of bad habits and reactivity. So please, dear reader, recognize that you're not alone in your idealism. Balancing commitments and maintaining good habits under stress is certainly a struggle. I will explore the various "traps" I fell into that hurt my ability to find balance. I hope my story will help you to prepare for your own challenges.

Stress is the fundamental issue. Most of these other behaviors are poor substitutes for proper stress management. Managing stress is easier said than done. I can give you a bunch of advice—tell you what stress-management experts say—but I can also tell you that sticking to a plan is harder than making a plan. Life will punch you in the mouth, and despite my best advice and your best preparation, it will hurt. But I can also tell you that everyone who has overcome something truly challenging has grown through the process.

I set my expectations for myself too high and believed I could do it all. I believed I could be everything to everyone and did not mentally accept that I would have to ruthlessly prioritize to live up to my ideal in any of my pursuits. I would advise you to write down all the commitments and aspirations that you have. If you generate this list while carefree, warm, and enjoying a beautiful summer day, you will likely be overly optimistic about all that you can balance. Dreaming about success is easier than the disciplined work required to achieve it.

PLAN: Pick up your pen again. Write out your commitments and goals for the next three months and rank-order them. What are you going to do if reality punches you in the mouth? When push comes to shove, what are your priorities?

I would create time to revisit this list of intended goals and confirm that they're your priorities. They are all important to you and, ideally, you will accomplish them all, but that's not a game plan.

In hindsight, I would have:

- Reduced my course load to the minimum necessary to graduate

- Set aside time to study and complete my academic work and refused to schedule over that time

- Notified all my other organizations that I would be taking a step back to prioritize the presidency

- Prioritized my exercise routine over everything but my service and recruited a friend to hold me accountable and train with me

- Scheduled in specific time at multiple points in the week to journal, unplug from technology, reflect, and think proactively

My friend Greg Corrado, who served as vice president '13-'14 of our student government and now works at Google as a deal expert, emphasized the importance of partnerships to manage stress:

> If you have a strong partnership and effectively delegate responsibilities, your stress is automatically cut in half, or even more. It seems to almost be a law of the universe.
>
> This understanding of the importance of effective partnerships has been valuable in all of my roles and enabled me to manage more and more responsibility.

Furthermore, considering I was working with an exceptional team of people, I could have better delegated tasks, asked for help, and prioritized my efforts to where I was most effective.

COFFEE COFFEE

Do you like coffee? I love coffee. I have been drinking it regularly, although not daily, since I was fourteen.

Or perhaps you prefer tea, soda, energy drinks, or some other method of caffeine consumption. Either way, please know that I share your likely appreciation for a nice caffeinated drink.

However, I have found that stress encourages me to abuse caffeine. I'll feel overwhelmed by my to-do list or a last-minute request and decide I need to grab another coffee, regardless of how much I've already had. This habit was particularly true during my senior year of college, during which I consumed an excessive amount every single day.

Throughout my senior year, I would regularly be upset, stressed, and experiencing feelings of self-loathing. I began to have a near-weekly ritual of heading to the dining hall and ordering a massive portion of lo mein, beef and broccoli, and orange chicken. The greasy food would taste so good for the first few bites, but then it would begin to drain me of my energy. I would chase this damaging meal with a no-sugar Monster energy drink, packed with 240 milligrams of caffeine. This beverage is essentially a sweet-tasting version of a cold-brew coffee, an excessive amount of caffeine.

I would sit in my windowless office with the door closed, feeling an odd combination of too-full-to-function and absolutely wired, the glow of my screen illuminating the bags under my eyes and my black Audio Technica M50Xs resting over my ears, playing fast electronic music. I would open Gmail and see all the non-urgent emails I had avoided for the last nine hours. I would then proceed to do a batch of email responses, working through over 100 emails during the next hour or so.

I hope this message finds you well… Sounds great, let's discuss more at our meeting next week… Attached is a copy of the agenda… I hope you have a wonderful weekend!… Thank you for your feedback. I will forward your message to…

Sincerely, Sincerely, Sincerely, Sincerely, Sincerely, Sincerely,
Grant   Grant   Grant   Grant   Grant   Grant

The minutes I saved by batching my emails did little to restore any balance to my life. None of the people I was emailing would know that I was struggling to keep my life under control, as my messages remained upbeat and warm.

The research suggests that people have mixed experiences using caffeine when faced with a stressful situation.[26] You may have a different relationship with caffeine and be able to avoid the downsides of excessive use. I hoped in sharing this story to highlight the potential to fall into patterns of substance abuse when confronted with excessive stress.

STRENGTH DRAINING

As I mentioned earlier, I only made it to the gym one time during that entire year. As soon as my environment changed, I lost my gym habit. I went from working out three days every week to not exercising for months at a time. I now believe that regular exercise is the most important habit.

It is easy for people to believe that they are too busy to exercise. Most people would find it absurd if someone said they were too busy to drink water. Fewer would find the same statement about exercising to be strange. I now believe that both of these are absurd statements, and I encourage every leader, and human, to prioritize a sustainable exercise routine.

We will explore concrete ways to build and maintain these habits in chapter nine. I just wanted to highlight it in this section because my lack of exercise was one of my biggest

26 (Richards and Smith 2015)

mistakes. Creating space for and prioritizing exercise is critical, especially when others are relying on you to show up and bring your best every single day.

SOCIAL MEDIA STRUGGLES

As I mentioned before, social media was pivotal to our administration's success. I ended up using my own personal Facebook account to engage the student body in the student government's various functions. Doing so enabled me to keep a finger on the pulse of the student body, engage students in opportunities to provide feedback to administrators, communicate about our values and initiatives, and wield student sentiment to lobby for changes. However, social media brought with it a host of other problems.

Advice to someone who's new to managing a public social media account:

- Don't let it take over your life; you have other commitments and priorities

- Automate posts when possible by using third-party apps or built-in functions

- Set aside specific times to respond to feedback to avoid constant usage

- Remove the apps from your phone or utilize tools to monitor and limit your usage

After making posts, I would neurotically check to ensure that the message was well-received. I had just gotten my first smart phone and lacked any consciousness about how it could dominate my life. The feedback from my posts conditioned me to be sensitive to the feedback of my peers, most of whom were fundamentally strangers. This mindset warped my sense of reality in many ways. The people who are super-users of social media, and the internet more generally, are not a representative population. Research shows that 1 percent of all users produce close to all of the content on most online platforms—and yet there I was, thinking that the people I was interacting with on there were the majority, that they best represented my constituents.[27]

When you take on the role of a leader, one of your most important functions is communicating with your members, audience, and users. Our contemporary social media culture is new and dynamic. I would advise every leader to think about how they can use these tools in productive and responsible ways.

---

27   (van Mierlo 2014)

PUBLIC POLITICS, MY BAD HOBBY

My problems with social media were compounded by the ferocity of internet politics at the time of my presidency. My term as president ran for the duration of the 2016 primaries. Throughout college, I had become more interested in public policy and politics. I am sure some of you can relate to how I became obsessed with following the headlines, tweets, and polls.

Overall, I would not advise any student leader to become so gripped by national politics during their service. My behavior, particularly weighing in on various policy discussions on Facebook, certainly alienated many strangers and created unnecessary tensions between me and people who otherwise supported me. In retrospect, my fixation on politics was a terrible use of my time that drained me emotionally. At the time, I thought I had a responsibility to be an outspoken advocate. But as time has passed, I have come to primarily view my behavior as immature and naive.

You need to figure out how to balance your desire to engage in hobbies, be authentic to yourself, and prioritize your responsibilities as a leader. If you are going to be the leader of a political group, you will be expected to be outspoken in favor of the values of your tribe. However, if your role involves you serving and collaborating with people who have a variety of perspectives, I would advise you to think carefully about what needs to be said publicly.

It is easy for people these days to believe that they must post and publish every thought that they have. In fact, such behavior is not necessary. As I mentioned earlier, only a small amount of people engage in such an activity.

BURNOUT

By the end of my term as president, I was absolutely burnt out. I needed constant coffee to keep my energy levels up. I was chronically checking my phone. Facebook. Email. Snapchat. GroupMe. Facebook. Repeat. I would struggle to fall asleep and curse myself for my coffee consumption, my lack of exercise, and my failure to live up to my ideal. I felt like a shell of my former self. I had lost control over my life. I had many new skill sets and a lot of people liking my posts on social media, but I didn't know what I wanted or what truly mattered to me. I had lost myself in the demands that others placed on me and my inability to properly manage the stress. Fundamentally, I was depressed and unhealthy.

Fortunately, I was able to start my road to recovery that summer. I was selected as a recipient of the Evans Lam Scholarship for Hong Kong and China. This award enabled me to travel to Hong Kong and study elementary Mandarin at the Chinese University of Hong Kong. Switching environments helped me to process my experiences from a different perspective.

While in Hong Kong, I entered a period of my life that was much more introverted. I decided not to make a bunch of new friends. I abstained from going out and partying. I relaxed and enjoyed the calm of a lack of responsibilities. I focused on learning as much Mandarin as I could. I explored Hong Kong alone. I ate delicious, authentic Chinese food—a significant improvement over the orange chicken I had been hate-eating. I started journaling, meditating, and going to the gym. I reflected and meditated on all that I had experienced and accomplished over the past year.

One evening, I was distraught and could not sleep. Decisions I had made during the flurry of my presidential term kept replaying in my head. I decided to pull out my journal and write down a list of every meaningful event and activity that I could remember from that past year. When I was done, I had a list of over forty things. Addressing the incoming freshmen, the surprise twenty-first birthday my friends planned for me, presenting to the university's board of trustees, spring break in Miami, and so much more.

This practice was valuable because it enabled me to gain a greater awareness of and internalize all that I had experienced. I had hurt myself and burned myself out, but my life had been deeply meaningful. That year taught me so much and gave me opportunities and relationships that are critical to who and where I am today. In fact, I almost certainly would not have decided to apply for the Take Five program, a fully funded fifth year of undergraduate studies where you complete a proposed curriculum, or started my role at iZone had I not run and won my race to be student body president.

While this chapter has been focused on the pain I experienced as a result of my decision to take responsibility, as well as my poor management of the associated stress, you should understand that I have no regrets.

As a leader, you will need to develop your own brand of pragmatism. While systems and habits can enable you to operate at a high level, life will not go as planned. You will be confronted by tough choices with no good options. Leaders are doers, and to get anything done, you need to make decisions, take action, and accept responsibility. You will experience times when this responsibility is painful. You will need to reframe and figure out how to incorporate your losses and struggles into your own story of personal growth.

Similar to other aspects of leadership, you need to embrace your agency and communicate your vision forward. The facts are what they are, but your story about them will influence your trajectory. On the other side of this experience, I felt humbled, self-aware, and confident in my ability to better manage future stress and greater responsibility. In chapter nine, I will dive deep into the habits and systems I've used to avoid these traps and perform at a higher level.

I learned from my experience and was able to mitigate and avoid these problems in my future pursuits:

- Phone addiction
- Antisocial internet usage
- Time management
- Poor diet
- Lack of exercise
- Damage to relationships

I was able to rebuild myself and integrate all I had learned into a new story for myself. It was not an easy process, but continuing to suffer was not an option. You might not find my experience relatable, but you will have your own unique struggles as you continue to lead. This lesson might be one that needs to be earned, rather than learned.

REFLECT (preferably on paper): Are you currently feeling overwhelmed by your commitments? What bad habits are you using to cope with the stress? How might you reduce the amount of stress that you're experiencing?

CHAPTER 5

ALL MODELS ARE WRONG, SOME ARE USEFUL

———

To be careless in making decisions is to naively believe that a single decision impacts nothing more than that single decision, for a single decision can spawn a thousand others that were entirely unnecessary or it can bring peace to a thousand places we never knew existed.

—CRAIG D. LOUNSBROUGH, FLECKS OF GOLD ON A PATH OF
STONE: SIMPLE TRUTHS FOR LIFE'S COMPLEX JOURNEY[28]

———

28   ("A Quote From Flecks Of Gold On A Path Of Stone" 2019)

Your effectiveness as a leader will result from the quality of your decision-making. Throughout this chapter, I will introduce you to a variety of frameworks that have changed how I think about decisions in theoretical discussions, my personal life, and as a leader.

In this chapter we will consider:

- Decision-making with incomplete information and uncertainty

- The importance of accountability and feedback for any leader

- The significance of scale when considering different types of problems

- The impact of goals and conscious priming in your performance and perception of opportunities

When referring to something as *complex* throughout this chapter, I mean it has the qualities of being:

- dynamic
- unpredictable
- interdependent
- multivariable

The economy is a great example of a complex system. The yield, or interest rate, of bonds affects savings and investment decisions, which affects employment, which affects wages, which affects consumer spending, which affects people's feelings about the world, which affects the price of stocks, etc. The complexity of this system makes accurate prediction impossible. Traders can still make money from buying and selling assets, but they are taking a risk every time; there is no certainty.

Similarly, think of a game of pool. When a cue ball is launched into the other balls to "break" and start the game, we cannot predict the trajectory and effect of the ball, because of the complexity involved in trying to model all of the relevant factors: the angles, the speed of the ball, the moisture in the air, the condition of the balls, the interplay between each of the balls and the table, etc.[29]

Now think of a company like SpaceX. I have an extremely limited understanding of physics, and my high school physics grades would confirm that. However, my gut instinct would have been that creating a perfect model of the pool example would be simple compared to the challenges that SpaceX faces. One of them is literally rocket science.

---

29 (Freiburger 2014)

Developing a model of the impact of a cue ball seems like an experiment you could conduct with a pool table, some sensors, a few engineers, and a powerful computer. Launching a rocket sounds like it would require an army of engineers, billions and billions of dollars of equipment, and innumerable third-party approvals. The part about rocket launches is true, while the part about the pool example is wildly incorrect.

The difference in these two examples is the level of complexity required to solve the problem. In the pool example, you need accurate information about a near infinite amount of variables to be able to compute a solution that will be anywhere close to accurate. If you gave a team the set-up that I mentioned before and asked them to create a model, their model would likely end up being worse than a prediction by a random person who had never played pool before.[30]

In the SpaceX example, while the company needs to account for perhaps hundreds or thousands of variables, the number is still finite. SpaceX is vulnerable to an important, unknown variable causing a launch to fail, but it can generate an economically viable success rate through diligence, world-class engineering, and risk management. While any individual launch risks not being successful, SpaceX can harness the

---

30 (Freiburger 2014)

power of technology and human talent to reduce its chance of failure and strive to change the trajectory of humanity.[31]

So, what can a game of pool and a space launch teach you about leadership?

Since all models of complex systems are imperfect, we cannot predict the specific outcome of the decisions we make as leaders. However, to solve complex problems, we still need to use imperfect models. As SpaceX's success demonstrates, an imperfect model can enable us to navigate uncertainty. As leaders, we must understand that we need to take risks, and when our decisions do not produce the intended results, we must accept responsibility.

MY LIFE AS AN UNDERGRADUATE ARMCHAIR EXPERT

While I was in college, I am pretty sure that I almost drove my family insane.

In studying economics and public policy, I was exposed to a never-ending stream of theories and models. After I was exposed to one and understood the thinking behind it, I would talk about it with my family members whenever I

---

31   (Fernholz 2019)

saw them: over lunch, coffee, on long car rides, on short car rides—there was no escaping my desire to talk through what I was learning.

Years later, I've stopped talking like I would be the wise, benevolent dictator of some utopian future. (My family and friends are grateful.) But what I've developed is a necessary skepticism of the models I used to consider infallible. Solving complex problems is more challenging than I was led to believe when I was an undergraduate. Here's what I mean:

In my Economics 101 course, I was taught about the inefficacy of the minimum wage and how it was a universally bad idea. Here is a brief characterization of the talking points present in a typical discussion between two undergraduate armchair experts on the merits of a minimum wage:

- Raising the minimum wage will raise wages that some workers receive. However, other workers will lose their jobs or be unable to find work, as businesses cannot justify paying those workers at the new minimum wage. The net effect will be a decrease in economic growth and greater unemployment.

- Employers in various sectors of the economy may be able to collude to keep workers' wages artificially low. However, minimum wage is not the best way to solve that problem, as a minimum wage will negatively affect hiring decisions in businesses where this is not an issue. This collusion is not a problem in areas where businesses are in fierce competition for competent employees.

- Workers are consumers, and those who do not benefit from the minimum wage will be penalized by the higher cost of goods that result from higher labor costs.

- Small businesses would be harmed as they will be unable to compete with large multinational corporations who have greater access to cash and can operate at a loss or invest in technology, while mom-and-pop shops go out of business. These large corporations will be able to increase long-run profits by raising prices after they destroy their competition.

- This policy will accelerate the shift toward automation of various tasks, as higher labor costs encourage businesses to seek automated solutions.[32]

While most or even all of the above clauses may have some validity, this discussion does not account for the fallibility of our models or the importance of the human element of policymaking. To say that a minimum wage policy is universally good or bad would imply that we live in a world where we can

---

32 (Lee 2019)

compute something like the pool problem. It assumes that economists have determined that, in all possible scenarios, a minimum wage policy would result in a net loss for "workers." Like perfectly predicting the cue ball's trajectory, such a determination is impossible.

Our world is more similar to the SpaceX example, to continue the analogy.

SpaceX needs rigorous thinking and incomplete models to make decisions about its rocket launches. When mistakes occur based on those models, however expertly done, SpaceX and Elon Musk must accept responsibility for the outcome.

From that realization, we can reframe the tribalistic Economics 101 discussion.

Now, let's consider this from a different lens. What if we had a global minimum wage policy, where no locality could permit someone to accept a lower wage?

This theoretical global legislature could set the minimum wage at some extremely low value. Let's assume it helps the globally lowest paid workers by increasing their hourly wage by 10 percent. This policy would do nothing to impact the wages of workers who were already earning more than this new global minimum wage.

At the other extreme, the global legislature could set the minimum wage at a globally high value. If the minimum wage were $16, this choice would leave most of the global population unemployed, or more likely choosing to ignore the decree of this inconsiderate One World Government. The people of Warsaw, Poland, may want a minimum wage of 15 Polish złoty (PLN) per hour, while the people of Arlington, Virginia, might not want a minimum wage at all.

The optimal solution would be one where those affected can hold a leader accountable for the decisions they make. If increases in the minimum wage yield less income inequality and improve the local economy, that outcome is great. If they lead to greater unemployment, drive up the cost of living, and convince people to leave the area, that's a tragedy. Leaders have to experience the consequences of their decisions and be directly held accountable.

Many mainstream policy discussions ignore the complexity of our world and disregard the importance of accountability in our leaders. Excluding decisions about the legality of immoral practices, such as slavery, discrimination, etc., or the violation of civil rights, laws should be controlled as close to home as possible. The more local a leader is, the more easily they can be held accountable and the more likely they are to be directly affected by their own policy. We should all want the chef to eat their own cooking.

If you live in Albuquerque, New Mexico, you can more easily march on City Hall than on Capitol Hill. Politicians who pass laws that impact the economic life of communities should viscerally experience the effects on the community, whether that's prosperity or the closing of mom-and-pop shops on Main Street.

Yes, some policies must be handled at the national or international level. But we should localize our attempts to solve problems as close to home as possible. That may mean Washington, D.C., but it may mean the town of Honeoye Falls, New York. Any policy, in a well-functioning state, should only be enacted if it is good for the government's constituents. And, in a democratic state, this practice would ideally be reflected in election results.

LEADING LOCALLY

My work for student government taught me about the importance of accountability and feedback for any leader. The college is responsible for providing numerous services to students: dining options, housing, busing, study spaces, and more. Students I talked with would often be upset about the quality of many of these services or changes that had been made.

Before I had discussions with the people in charge of administering these services, I did not realize how much of a disconnect existed between a student's understanding of why a decision was made and administrators' understanding of how their decisions impacted the user experience. Sometimes the student understanding of the reasoning behind a choice was lacking. Other times the administrators simply had not received feedback about the impact of their choices. By the time I finished working at iZone, I had experienced these issues from the perspective of a student user, a student advocate, and a college administrator.

When iZone first launched at the end of 2017, we were operating out of a fluorescent closet in the heart of our college library. This time enabled us to learn more about students' needs, conduct deep research on best-practices, and experiment with our programs and organizational model. The following fall semester, we officially launched our program with the completion of the renovation of our future home, a beautiful 12,000-square-foot space. Unfortunately, in order to renovate the space, we needed to close it down for the entirety of the spring 2018 semester. Students, especially the seniors about to graduate, were furious about this decision. Students even circulated a petition to compel the student government to convince us to not close the space.

We realized that, while we had published our reasoning on our website and social media and told students at our events, we needed to create a space and time for students to talk with us in person. We hosted an open house in our future home, brought cookies, and set up various stations with renderings of the renovated iZone, information about our program, and little branded pocket notebooks. While the students were angry, it was much easier to get them to understand our reasoning once we could talk to them face to face.

We were conscious of the effects of the decision to renovate the space, but we were unable to wait until the summer because the renovations required more than three months to complete. In fact, the renovations were not complete until the week before the fall freshman orientation, despite our decision to begin construction in January. We only had one week to move into our space before we began our first semester.

This example reveals that many problems stem from a lack of communication between the various stakeholders. This lack of communication may occur despite the interest of both parties in sharing their perspectives.

Sometimes, the best way to facilitate feedback is by ensuring the decision-makers are also users. For example, I always believed that the dining services at the University of Rochester were excellent. They were responsive to any feedback that we provided to them, explained the reasoning behind their decisions, and literally ate their own cooking. When I was serving as president, I would see, Cam Schauf, director of dining services, at Starbucks and in one of the dining halls every day.

The necessity of accountability and feedback is clear when we're operating at a smaller scale. Not only are they important when you're operating a service or serving in government, but they are critical to any organization. It should be clear who is responsible for the various functions of your organization, and you should have systems to ensure decision-makers receive regular feedback.

WRITE: Reflect on the various teams you've been a part of, work or otherwise. How functional was the organization? Was it clear what your responsibilities were? Are there any actions you could take to apply this principle of accountability and feedback to your life right now?

Once you internalize the unpredictability, randomness, and complexity of our reality, you will become endlessly frustrated by the claims of people who believe they can predict the future. Our world is full of people who advocate for the universal good or bad of policies by cherry-picking examples and speaking generically. A Democrat will point to the Bush tax cuts and say, "See? Tax cuts do not work." A Republican will present the murder rate statistics of Chicago and say, "See? Gun control does not work."

The specific claims about the efficacy of the Bush tax cuts or gun safety measures in Chicago are certainly debatable. But it is less debatable that one example is sufficient to make a universal argument about the validity of tax cuts or gun safety measures. This type of argument is a form of tribalism that will reduce your ability to think critically about our world. It might be easy, it may feel good, but it is not what our world needs from our leaders.

PERCEIVING AND PLANNING

Throughout my education, I always felt a bit jealous of my peers who were sure about their career paths. While many of these people changed their plans as they got more experience or did not get a high enough MCAT score, clearly having a vision for their future was incredibly valuable.

I have personally struggled to find a purpose I could organize my life around. However, I have gained some clarity as I have gotten more work and life experience. While I still do not have a specific cause or project I wish to dedicate my entire self to, I now know that I want to leverage my interpersonal, communication, and leadership skills to help lead and empower teams to solve problems big and small. My hope is that the publication of this book will connect me with other definite optimists who will want to collaborate on challenging problems.

For those of you with a clear plan, this section may only help you to bolster your confidence in the benefits of having one. For those of you who cannot focus on one topic, problem, or purpose, we can use this part as an opportunity to introspect and come up with a bad plan.

We see only a sliver of the world. Our bodies cannot process all the stimuli around us and still function at a high level. Human beings evolved over generations and generations by natural selection. Our survival has required humans to be able to intensely focus and prioritize awareness of some aspects of our environment while ignoring others.

A few months ago, I woke up at 6 a.m. to go exercise before work. While half-asleep, I wandered out my door and began my morning commute. As I walked to the gym, I hardly noticed any of my environment. I did not see the stop sign at the end of my street. I did not see my neighbor's grey Toyota Camry in their driveway. I did not see the cigarette butts strewn along the sidewalk. Suddenly, I jumped a foot in the air and was fully alert. My attention was focused intensely on the sidewalk right where I was about to step. What had startled me? A black cable that vaguely looked like a snake.

Current research shows that humans are actually more attuned to stimuli that share characteristics with snakes.[33] Furthermore, we are generally more engaged and affected by negative than positive stimuli.[34] While seeing something beautiful might make us happy for a moment, being bitten by a poisonous snake could mean death.

This negativity bias is exploited by the media we consume. Often, news stories are chosen to amplify alarm and headlines to provoke outrage. Politicians speak to people's fears and concerns. The best marketing and content pull at our emotions to keep us paying attention and watching. An understanding of this phenomena is insufficient to reduce its effect. It is hardwired into our biology and what it means to be human. It's the snake on the sidewalk.

However, we can harness our body's ability to prioritize stimuli by intentionally priming ourselves to view the world through a desired lens. If you have ever learned a new word or fact and then seen something relevant soon after, you have experienced the power of this phenomenon.

Religions, such as sects of both Christianity and Buddhism, have daily prayers or rituals that have a similar effect. You

---

33 (Öhman and Mineka 2003)
34 (Rozin and Royzman 2001)

may start and end your day by focusing on what you're most grateful for in your life: your family, your health, the opportunity to make a difference in people's lives, your best friends, your neighbors, and the basic necessities of life. Concentrating your focus on these positive aspects of your life primes you to experience the world in a way that emphasizes these priorities.

So, how does this relate to goal-setting?

During my four years of cross-country running, I was fortunate to have a world-class coach, Bernie Gardner. I did not appreciate it at the time because I had no discipline but, although he was a strict coach, he was dedicated to his craft and incorporated the best practices of Olympic coaches. Every year, he would tell us the story of an Olympian who spent at least an hour every day simply visualizing the contest he was preparing for. This Olympian does train hard, but his edge comes from his visualization, which enables him to secure a gold medal and a new world record.

> Lyndon Rush, one of Canada's bronze medalists in bobsledding, described the importance of visualization to his training in an interview with the *New York Times*:

I've tried to keep the track in my mind throughout the year. I'll be in the shower or brushing my teeth. It just takes a minute, so I do the whole thing or sometimes just the corners that are more technical. You try to keep it fresh in your head, so when you do get there, you are not just starting at square one. It's amazing how much you can do in your mind.[35]

At one extreme, you have people who have a clear purpose. They are successful in organizing their lives around a central goal. That might be raising your children to be happy and healthy, attending medical school and becoming a doctor, qualifying for the Olympics, or anything else. On the other extreme, you have people who are nihilistic and aimless—people who have no guiding focus or feeling of purpose.

Humans feel positive emotion because of the direction in which they are heading relative to their goals and ideals.[36] To overcome the bad in your life, it is critical that you generate positive emotion by progressing toward self-defined goals.

He who has a why can bear any how.

—FRIEDREICH NIETZSCHE[37]

When your life is totally focused on one goal, your relationship to the entire world changes. If you are committed to

---

35 (Clarey 2014)
36 (Ramnerö and Törneke 2014)
37 ("Friedrich Nietzsche Quotes" 2019)

winning the national championship in a sport, you begin to experience life through that lens: An invitation to a party transforms from a great opportunity to socialize with strangers and friends into an obstacle, a temptation that must be overcome. An advertisement for an organic, no-whey protein shake might go from irrelevant to engaging and attractive. Conversation with a close friend might be more likely to venture toward their college roommate whose best friend was the national champion from Poland.

Viewing the world through a lens focused on your goals and values will enable you to make better decisions and see opportunities that you might otherwise have ignored. If you are not conscious of the relationship between your goals and the information you're exposed to, you're less likely to identify and take concrete steps toward reaching those goals.

Later in this book, in chapter nine, we will discuss tactics and ideas for orienting yourself around habits and systems that will enable you to progress toward your desired ideal. Regardless of whether you already have orienting goals, let's take some time to reflect on our values through writing.

WRITE: *Reflecting on your values and motivations is critical for success in any goal-setting process. Please consider exploring the following prompts:*

- Write about a time when you felt highly motivated. What did that feel like? What drove you to be motivated? Is there anything about that experience that you could replicate toward a future goal?

- Write about a time when you felt most alive.

- During what activities does time seem to fly by? Are there any commonalities between these activities?

- If you won $10 million (after taxes) in the lottery, what would you do with it?

- What if you had to use the money to help others but could not simply give it away?

CHAPTER 6

IZONE MAFIA

The gap year between my time as president and my time starting at iZone challenged me in a completely different way. While my time as president had been chaotic and led me to burn out, I found it deeply meaningful. The absence of a formal role in my community, after a year of hyper-involvement and service, created a huge contrast.

My life was low-stress, but it felt empty.

That contrast emphasized to me how much I value having a social function within my community. My gap year was valuable in that it gave me time to think, reflect, and rebuild, but by the end of it, I was more than ready to commit myself to a project I believed in.

Serving as the founding community manager of iZone at the University of Rochester gave me new opportunities to develop my understanding of leadership and management. It was the first leadership role where I was able to design the organization, help build the foundation, and dedicate myself full time, without classes getting in the way. Also new to me was access to a budget to pay our employees and the responsibility of managing our limited funds. Prior to that, I had been a student and my leadership roles and those of my collaborators had been strictly voluntary. In my role, I focused on empowering our team, managing our programming and marketing activities, and establishing an organizational model and culture that would transcend my time at iZone.

When you start any project, there are two initial questions to focus on:

- *What problem are you solving?*

- *Whose problem are you solving?*

Before I started in my role, the university had hired consultants to dive into these questions. They wanted to validate the concept of iZone before expending too many resources on it. As a student, I had supported the general concept of iZone and promoted opportunities for students to be interviewed and express their opinions.

Students and other stakeholders collectively identified a few problems:

- Lack of available space specifically designed to facilitate collaboration and projects-based learning

- Absence of a robust community for students to find collaborators or associate with others pursuing extracurricular projects and ventures

- Insufficient resources to help students get started, troubleshoot problems, and connect with collaborators throughout the university's network

With a general idea of who our target users were and what problems needed solving, the Barbara J. Burger iZone at the University of Rochester Libraries was funded and founded.

I know what you're thinking: *But why "iZone"?*

iZone's name was created in consultation with our founding donor, Barbara J. Burger, who serves as president of Chevron Technology Ventures. The "i" has many meanings: ideas, inquiry, innovation, imagination...and:

"iZone is a creative problem-solving space, program, and community designed to empower students to explore and imagine ideas for social, cultural, community, and economic impact."[38]

This statement was the formal description of iZone when I began my role there. To describe ourselves in a simple sentence, we began to say, "iZone is the first stop for students with big ideas." With our mission articulated, our core problems to solve identified, and a clear budget established, the rest was up to our team. My boss, Julia Maddox, hired me to serve as the founding "community manager" and we got to work to "Make It Happen."

During my two years at iZone, I also advised students on their projects. In their early stages, I continued to pose these important questions: *What problem are you solving? Whose problem is it?* We may often think we've had a genius idea and, if we have a bias for action, run with it and move forward as fast as possible. This passion and drive are critical but ultimately not sufficient. Creators who push forward without considering and answering these questions leave themselves vulnerable to working on ideas that do not solve their users' problems.

In iZone's case, our target users were students at the University of Rochester, and more specifically: passionate,

---

38 ("iZone" 2019)

high-agency, entrepreneurial, creative, and self-starting students. Not everyone who was a regular user checked all of those boxes, but most did, which made my job phenomenal and gave me a lot of optimism for our future.

Every day, our space was full of students from all over the world working and collaborating on a variety of projects. Some regular users would come and go all day, leaving for a coffee refill or class. Our yellow and blue booths, project rooms, and whiteboards were perpetually in use. Yes, students used our beautiful space as a place to study, socialize, and do their homework. But many of those students would stay to work on their personal projects and attend our events. Students even began to demand that we create a system to give preference to students working on ventures unrelated to their studies or student organizations.

I easily met several hundred students taking action to solve a problem that had captured their energy and attention. Their projects ranged from developing a peace studies curriculum for students to ease conflicts between tribes in their home country to a business that would help college staff and faculty find qualified, on-demand babysitters. Watching these projects grow from a half-formed idea to a prototype and beyond was all the validation I needed.

MAKING A MAFIA

Play long-term games with long-term people...if you want to be successful, you have to work with other people. And you have to figure out who can you trust, and who can you trust over a long, long period of time.

—NAVAL RAVIKANT, FOUNDER OF ANGELLIST[39]

Julia was the perfect person to be founding director—creative, high-energy, and persistent. These traits enabled her to develop a clear strategic mission and give our team the freedom to experiment, screw up, and thrive.

One of my responsibilities was hiring our student team. This task was great but challenging. Every time we sought applications, we identified more excellent candidates than we could hire. Rochester students are bright, hardworking, and come from all over the United States and world.

We made the strategic decision to create a student-powered program, and I believe it enabled all our early successes. Since we were creating this program at a college, we could reasonably hope that any student we hired would continue to work for us until they graduated. During the first hiring period, I ended up hiring four students, three of whom

---

39 (Ravikant 2019)

were first-years. Collectively, they had prior experience with leading projects and organizations, social media marketing, event-planning, web development, and leading workshops on design thinking.

As we headed into our second year and launched our space, we scaled up our team. Again, I focused on hiring the most qualified people who had the skills our team was lacking: videography, editing, and visual design, to name a few. I only hired people I could see myself collaborating with in life after iZone. Our resulting team was also diverse in every sense of the word, including in class year, gender, country of origin and ethnicity, major, and co-curricular involvement.

During the school year, our student employees made up the majority of all labor hours. They put together all our workshops and events, prototyped our student consulting model, advised their peers, and enabled them to connect with vital resources. We paid them for their time, but what we wanted from them was their energy, creativity, and heart.

To create extra value for my team, I needed them to understand that I was committed to continuing our relationships. Furthermore, both Julia and I recognized the importance of investing time and resources into their professional development. If we could help them to get excellent internships for the summer, not only would that help them, but our program would benefit from their greater competency and, in the long run, their networks. I still write them letters of recommendation, nominate them for awards, and connect them to people within my network. I also hope to find ways to continue collaborating over the course of my life.

Remember one of our principles of leadership in chapter three from Kouzes and Posner, "You Can't Do It Alone"?

In preceding chapters, I have referred to quotes, concepts, and ventures by Elon Musk and Peter Thiel. These two, along with Reid Hoffman, Luke Nosek, Ken Howery, and Keith Rabois constitute what is known as the Paypal Mafia. They all worked together to build, grow, and ultimately sell Paypal. Since that collaboration, each has gone on to find even greater influence and success. Paypal Mafia even has its own Wikipedia article.[40]

I want to create an iZone Mafia.

EPIC FAIL

The University of Rochester was a wonderful place to attend college—it challenged me in a lot of ways. However, one of its features is also one of its problems: many of the people

---

40 ("Paypal Mafia | Wikipedia" 2019)

who occupy its halls are overachievers and perfectionists. At iZone, we sought to help remedy this problem by launching a new event series: Screw Up Night.

Screw Up Night is an event at which selected guests and members of the audience have the opportunity to share a story of failure with the audience. Moralizing about the acceptability of failure and necessity of taking risks is not permitted. The event is meant to counter perfectionism, create an opportunity to practice public speaking, normalize failure and risk-taking, and generate a lot of laughs. The structure was the brain-child of Deniz Cengiz, one of the first-year students I hired during our first hiring cycle. The host of the event recruits administrators, professors, staff members, and other members of the community to kick off the event. They each address the crowd and tell their favorite story about a time they "screwed up."

There is laughter. There is applause. There are loud, clamorous cowbells (provided). After the selected speakers have set the tone and warmed up the stage, the floor is opened up to the crowd to tell their own stories. Without fail (*ba dum tss*), someone from the crowd steals the show by telling the most absurd story. The story with the loudest reaction gets something like a mock oversized check for $0,000,000 or a paper sash with "QUEEN OF FAILURE" written on it in sharpie.

The last Screw Up Night I was able to attend was the "Presidential Screw Up Night." It featured then-University of Rochester President Richard Feldman. The audience loved how President Feldman was willing to participate in the event. As we are believers in open source at iZone, I would highly encourage others to organize their own version of Screw Up Night.

Screw Up Night is just one example of the fun sort of contributions we brought to the University of Rochester community. We also:

- Designed and ran summer crash courses for high school students in design thinking, pitching, and user research, which they were made to apply to solve problems for a set of users

- Collaborated with our college's admissions office on fun programs for accepted students to encourage them to enroll

- Developed tool kits and a resource database for our student consultants to help their peers overcome obstacles and connect them to partners, funding opportunities, and information

- Facilitated workshops for departments throughout the college to help them to empathize with their users and troubleshoot problems

OUR INVALUABLES

My biggest takeaway from my time at iZone was the importance of culture in building any high-functioning organization. In an attempt to preserve the cultural elements we found helpful to our work, members of our team collaborated to record our "invaluables." Our goal was to create a set of fun, pithy statements that we could say to remind each other of our shared values:

Make It Happen: *We have the power to realize our ideas and overcome challenges. At iZone, we take ownership for our work and confront problems head on. Taking ownership often involves finding the right collaborators to help you.*

This invaluable is the one that immediately had the most buy-in on our team. Everyone on our team valued the opportunity to take ownership and be biased toward action. This approach empowered our employees to advocate for and execute on their own ideas. I would tell our team, "Feel free to solve any problem you identify, just don't forget to tell me about your solution." And they did just that. From troubleshooting network problems to implementing new ways to expand our email list, they used their autonomy to move our program forward.

Play Is Powerful: *We believe that play does not detract from our ability to achieve our mission but rather improves our* *chances of success. Our work, events, and workshops should never be boring.*

To get people interested, iZone needed to be fun. From the beginning, Julia and I wanted to create a program differentiated from many other learning experiences on campus and demonstrate that problem-solving and hard work can be fun. Not only did this mindset bring joy to the people who interacted with our programs, but it made our day-to-day experience wonderful and helped us build rapport as a team.

Do Less, Better: *We have limited time and resources to achieve our mission. If we are going to operate at the highest level, we need to focus our energy on the best opportunities and experiments. To do that, we need to be able to say "no" (politely).*

You may have noticed that iZone was engaged in a lot of distinct activities (and that was only the short of it). We committed to a lot of experiments and collaborations during the first three semesters of our program. At times, doing so led to our team becoming overwhelmed by a barrage of deadlines and commitments. "Do Less, Better" became a mantra to counteract our impulse to overcommit ourselves and emphasize the need to prioritize.

Keep It Human: *It's important for us to recognize our own humanity and that of the people we're serving or collaborating* *with. Prefer to speak face to face, ask people about their weekend, and don't be afraid to smile or wave when you see someone in a different context.*

As our responsibilities scaled, we needed more formal processes to continue to deliver on our promises to our community. But we didn't want those processes to be viewed as substitutes for genuine human interactions. We needed to make sure that our team continued to interact with our users and each other in ways that emphasized interpersonal relationships and empathy.

Better Every Time: *iZone will never be perfect. We must take the time to record any problems we notice or feedback we receive and take action to improve.*

Feedback was crucial for improving our offerings and prioritizing our time, energy, and attention. After you've worked all day, finished an event at ten at night, and spent twenty minutes cleaning up afterward, it's tempting to just say goodnight and leave. We created this invaluable so we could remind each other to take an extra four minutes to document what went well, what could be improved, and any ideas for future experiments to run. We wanted to emphasize that our program exists to best serve our users, not for our egos.

My personal experience working at iZone was distinct from my time serving as president. I created and maintained habits that enabled me to manage stress and perform at a high level nearly every day. I had learned from my prior mistakes and created space to introspect, take care of my health, and be a good friend, all of which enabled me to lead proactively. While we had times when we had to put all hands on deck to meet a deadline, Julia and I made time to think deeply about our strategic mission, reprioritize, and imagine how our decisions would create more opportunities for iZone in the future.

I should emphasize that iZone is still in its infancy, as of the time of writing. While I am proud of the current state of the program, I know that our team is currently working to build off our foundation and take it to the next level. In fact, our program should gain more users, engagement, and buy-in every year for the next three years even if our team were only maintaining what we created.

Every freshman orientation is a critical opportunity for the program to capture the attention and engage the eager first-year students. Every accepted students' day recruits more students who view themselves as problem-solvers, artists, or entrepreneurs. I am looking forward to checking in during the summer of 2021 to see where iZone is after four years.

When I made the decision to leave iZone, I did not do so because I was burnt out or no longer enjoying my job. In fact, I was happy, healthy, and loved my role and the environment. I left because I knew that my work there was done. While I would have been happy to continue to be in that positive environment, I knew the time had come for me to seek out a new challenge to test my skills and expand my understanding of myself and the world. After all, if I want to create an iZone Mafia, I need to take risks, expand my skill sets, and lead by example. It was time for my next adventure.

REFLECT: Do any of the organizations you belong to have their own version of invaluables? How effective are they at producing their desired outcome? Are they memorable and actionable?

CHAPTER 7

THE POWER
LAW OF YOU

There is a tension between deterministic and probabilistic models of our world. By deterministic, I mean the idea that our lives could be modeled in a way where each action will result in a knowable chain of reactions. In a deterministic model, there is no room for randomness. In a probabilistic model, our actions do not necessarily generate a knowable outcome and should instead be viewed as having a range of potential outcomes, which could theoretically be assigned probabilities.

Our experiences can be understood from both lenses. A story will help to clarify what I mean:

Ania made money from creating an internet business that sells and delivers a special green tea only grown in a specific village in China. After purchasing ads on a Silicon Valley influencer's podcast, her product became a viral sensation and the tea of choice for any highly productive(™) startup founder. She used the profits from her business to purchase a Tesla, the premiere electric vehicle at the time of writing. She values reducing her carbon footprint (and her locality produces most of its energy through its highly efficient nuclear plant).

One day, Ania was driving through the city to visit her relatives when another driver suddenly swerved into her car. Her Tesla was pushed off the road and totaled. Thankfully, both drivers emerged unharmed and her insurance covered the damages.

This incident could be viewed from a deterministic model of the world. Ania chose to drive a certain route at a specific speed and the other driver also took intentional actions that resulted in their collision.

On the other hand, we could also view this story from a probabilistic lens. Insurance companies think about Ania's story first and foremost from a probabilistic lens. They charge Ania a premium every month, which is a function of numerous factors (age, gender, previous accident history, car model, etc).

If an insurance company wants to stay profitable, it must first charge Ania at a rate that will enable the company to secure her business. If it was charging her much more than competing insurers, she would likely switch to one of its competitors.

Next, the insurance company must also charge her at a rate that reflects the risk of insuring her, or more simply the probability of her being in an accident and filing a legitimate claim. If the company believes Ania is a less risky driver than she actually is, her claims could exceed the total amount of money she has paid in premiums. An insurance company that fails to accurately assess the risk of insuring its clients will become unprofitable and go out of business.

Ania has agency to choose her route, speed, etc.; she can make decisions and has no intention of getting into an accident. However, the insurance company must model her driving experience by assigning a distribution of probabilities of various outcomes in order to charge her at a profitable rate. The story of Ania's unfortunate accident can in this way be modeled both deterministically and probabilistically. We live in an uncertain world, where randomness plays a critical role, and yet every decision we make is significant.

As leaders, we must recognize that our decisions will affect the world and change the future. At times, the results of our actions may appear to reflect what we anticipated, while at others unpredictable outcomes will result. The future is inherently uncertain, and a probabilistic understanding of the world can help us to think critically about a range of possible outcomes and inform our decision-making.

INEQUALITY AND POWER LAWS

One of the people who has most influenced my thinking is former Wall Street trader, philosopher, and best-selling author Nicholas Nassim Taleb. If you find some of the ideas about probability in this book interesting and useful, I highly recommend you read his collection of books, *Incerto*.

A main idea in one of the books from Taleb's *Incerto, The Black Swan,* is that the bell curve does not provide a valid model for many kinds of data and phenomena.

If you are a student, you will likely be most familiar with the bell curve from your experience taking tests. It is common for teachers and professors to grade exams on a [bell] curve. They will assign a certain amount of As, Bs, Cs, etc. based on the distribution of scores on the exam. This enables the teacher to avoid giving every student an A, on an easy exam, or giving every student an F, if the exam was designed for students with greater proficiency.

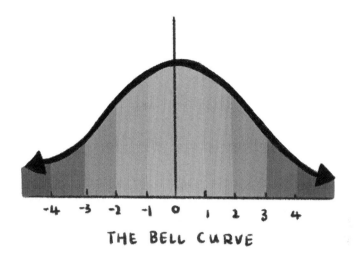

THE BELL CURVE

Certain sets of data do not fit inside this bell curve distribution. These data sets tend to be focused on domains related to money and social phenomena, rather than biology. We can model many of these kinds of distributions as an exponential growth curve, or "winner-take-most" or "winner-take-all" model. For example, you have likely heard that the top 1 percent of the wealthiest people in the United States owned 38.6 percent of all American wealth in 2016[41]—an example of this type of power law distribution.

---

41 (*Changes In U.S. Family Finances From 2013 To 2016: Evidence From The Survey Of Consumer Finances* 2017)

The power law curve looks something like this:

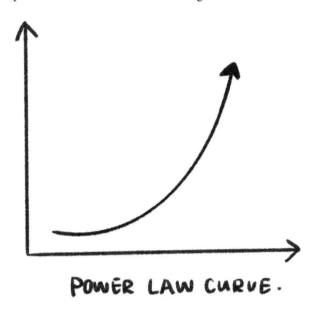

POWER LAW CURVE.

Any sufficiently advanced technology is indistinguishable from magic.

—SIR ARTHUR C. CLARKE, AUTHOR,
INVENTOR, AND FUTURIST[42]

In the case of, say, Mark Zuckerberg or Jeff Bezos, this tremendous wealth results from their ability to monetize the value their companies provide. They were able to not only create value, but also successfully convert it into profit. In

---

42 ("Arthur C. Clarke Quotes" 2019)

contrast, Jimmy Wales, the founder of Wikipedia, has created tremendous value for the world but did not implement a business model that would enable him to amass wealth in proportion to the value he created.[43]

We can also look at a historical example. George Eastman, with his company Eastman Kodak, popularized personal film cameras. These cameras radically expanded people's ability to capture photos and were critical to the mass adoption of photography as a consumer good. Eastman Kodak was a tremendously profitable company that captured large amounts of the value it created, through its monopoly on film production and processing. Due to Kodak's patents, they faced little to no competition for many years.

The proliferation of cameras has created immense value for society, and these products are now available globally. In my lifetime, I have experienced both disposable Kodak film cameras and the incredible, machine-learning-augmented Pixel 2 camera. The latter has enabled my brother to thoroughly document the childhoods of my niece and nephew. A low estimate suggests there may be 10,000 times the amount of photos and videos of their childhood than mine or my brother's.

---

43   (Cadwalladr 2014)

A company like Kodak can be cited as an example of both the tyranny of monopolies and the value created from technological innovation. At the time of writing, every smartphone now has a camera orders of magnitude more powerful than anything George Eastman could have hoped to create. While phone companies today compete at the margin to provide the best camera, a high-quality camera is a required feature for any smartphone. Commercial cell phone manufacturing is a highly competitive market with moderate profits, especially contrasted with Eastman Kodak's consumer film monopoly under George Eastman's leadership.

While Facebook and Amazon receive justifiable criticism for some of their business activities and the exorbitant wealth of their founders, their critics often ignore or overlook the value they have created. Facebook enables their users to communicate with their friends, family, and fans, facilitates distribution for independent news sources and other entrepreneurs, and encourages fundraising for thousands of nonprofit projects. Likewise, Amazon empowers many small businesses to expand their markets, supports new products and business opportunities through Amazon Web Services, and enables authors, like me, to get our content to our readers in person, on Kindle, or via Audible. You may have good reason to critique these firms, but the point of this section is to point out this tension that arises from innovation.

Inequality can result from innovation that provides immense value to our lives. The reality is that power law distributions exist and we should develop an understanding of the origins of these inequalities.

Another example of power laws can be found in search engine usage. In August 2019, Google's search engine was used for 93.14 percent of all mobile searches. The next largest search engine, Baidu, only accounted for 3.56 percent of mobile searches.[44] This dominance in search results enabled Google to generate 86.78 percent of all its revenues from Q3 2017 to Q3 2018. This distribution has been relatively stable over time.[45] In this example, we see that not only is there a power law distribution in the usage of these search engines but there is a power law in revenues generated internal to Google. While they have numerous other products, including the aforementioned Pixel phones, they account for a small fraction of their total revenues.

Recognizing the inequality the power law represents is critical to understanding our modern world. These distributions are an issue the next generation of leaders will have to grapple with as we work to build a more prosperous future. Obscuring and ignoring these inequalities is neither pragmatic nor

44   ("Search Engine Market Share" 2017)
45   (Rosenberg 2018)

moral. We need to continue to permit businesses, their customers, and their employees to benefit from the value they create, but we also need to develop institutions that are more effective at supporting those who do not directly prosper as a result of these innovations.

OWNING YOUR BRAND

One of the ways leaders can expand their influence in our smartphone society is by leveraging technology to distribute information to their fans and build their personal brand. While you don't need to have a public persona to be a leader, it certainly can expand your ability to influence and enable you to build connections and find opportunities.

Remember Ania and our earlier discussion of probabilistic models? With our understanding of the power law, we can now reflect on the relationship between power laws and a probabilistic model of the world.

When considering the power law curve and its applicability to social media following, you can interpret the x-axis as a distribution of probabilities. Most people are in the "long tail," or the far left of the curve, which is flat compared to the right tail of the distribution. The probability that you will become a viral success, or fall into the farthest right side of the curve, by using social media platforms is incredibly low. The average twitter user has 770 followers[46], 391 million accounts have zero followers[47], and Kanye West has 29.2 million followers[48]. On Instagram, 70 percent of users have less than 1,000 followers[49], while Kim Kardashian West has 148.9 million followers.[50]

In this world of power laws, concentrations of value will be captured disproportionately by a small subsection of our society. While wealthy people and businesses can allocate resources toward purchasing advertisements to increase their reach, I feel confident saying that no amount of money and advertisements would generate for me as large of a reach as Kanye West. I'd be a fool to bet on that changing someday.

However, the important part is that you and I can also leverage these platforms to boost our credibility and expand our reach. While there are significant winners at the top, there are also extreme distributions lower on the curve. In order to have the opportunity to climb and expand your reach, you need to at least be on the curve. Managing a public persona is certainly not for everyone, and social media may be harmful

---

46 (MacCarthy 2016)
47 (Murphy 2014)
48 ("Ye (@Kanyewest) On Twitter" 2019)
49 ("Instagram Follower Rates 2018" 2018)
50 ("Kim Kardashian West (@Kimkardashian) • Instagram" 2019)

to most users' lives, but you should at least be aware of the opportunity and the nature of the distribution.

One of the great aspects of your personal brand is that you do not need to sign any forms to own it. If you start tweeting videos of your art and they go viral, you will have the ability to capture additional value from that reach. To clarify, when I say value, I do not mean that you will necessarily be able to personally monetize your following. However, you will be able to amplify different stories, distribute your work, and influence others through this reach. The impact on your life of having this greater reach is unknowable, but we can think of it as increasing the probability of various outcomes.

And, let's be real, who needs a million followers anyway? Let alone 149 million.

999 REAL FANS

Lookin' for all my real friends
How many of us? How many of us are real friends
To real friends, 'til the reel end
'Til the wheels fall off, 'til the wheels don't spin

—KANYE WEST, "REAL FRIENDS"[51]

---

51 (West and Dolla $ign 2016)

This section is a synthesis of the essay "1,000 True Fans" by Kevin Kelly—author and former editor of *WIRED Magazine*—and the self-love exemplified by Kanye West.

Kelly's essay opens:

> To be a successful creator, you don't need millions. You don't need millions of dollars or millions of customers, millions of clients or millions of fans. To make a living as a craft person, photographer, musician, designer, author, animator, app maker, or entrepreneur, or inventor you need only thousands of true fans.[52]

The impetus for Kelly to write this essay was not a discovery of these power laws or the desire to simply write a contrarian essay during the globalization of celebrity. He decided to write his essay because of the emergence of networks like Facebook and Twitter, which were facilitating direct, instantaneous communication between creators and their fans. The ability to have a conversation with your fans changed the reality of what it meant to be a fan and opened new possibilities for how one could work full time as a creator.

---

52   (Kelly 2016)

Depending on your specialization and cost of living, you could potentially live off having 1,000 "true fans," or even fewer. These are fans who will purchase from or donate to you to support your craft because they love what you make and want you to focus your energy on creating.

If you lived in Rochester, New York, as a single bachelor, you could easily survive on $36,000 per year, assuming you could qualify for a low premium health care plan. If you can, then you would only need your 1,000 real fans to give you an average of $36 per year, or $3 per month, to cover all your expenses. As we've seen, both wealth and social media following fall into a power law distribution. The math—$36 per fan per year on average times 1,000 fans equals $36,000—is correct. However, in reality, you might have one fan who contributes a disproportionate amount of your total earnings.

If you've ever watched any of the top Twitch streamers—people who play video games full time—you will see this phenomenon. When Fortnite first came out, I would regularly watch Ninja play, and he would receive a consistent stream of $8 donations and always thanked each donor by name. Every time I watched him play, he would start losing it midstream: "Oh my god. Thank you so much. Really, thank you, thank you. Wow," and then you would see that one subscriber donated $1,000 to his stream. In an interview with ESPN, Ninja told them that $40,000 was the largest single donation he had received at one time.[53] That one donation is 5,000 times the size of those $8 donations.

Let's now consider our confident friend Kanye West. One of the greatest surprises of 2018 for me was that I became a giant Ye, or Kanye West fan. He produced albums for Pusha T and Nas, produced and performed *KIDS SEE GHOSTS* with Kid Cudi, and released *ye* all within the span of a few weeks. The high quality of this avalanche of albums prompted me to review his discography, and I probably listened to *KIDS SEE GHOSTS* over fifty times.

In particular, the song "Reborn" was exactly what I needed:

> I had my issues, ain't that much I could do
>
> But, peace is something that starts with me, with me
>
> At times, wonder my purpose
>
> Easy then to feel worthless
>
> But, peace is something that starts with me.[54]

---

53 (Webb 2018)
54 (Kids See Ghosts 2018)

I had liked some of Kanye's music in the past, but I never really understood why he had such devout fans. From the Taylor Swift "Imma let you finish" incident to listening to him sing "I Am A God," I just couldn't understand his extreme egotism.

My perspective changed when I heard Kanye in this BBC interview:

> If you're a Kanye West fan, you're not a fan of me. You're a fan of yourself. You will believe in yourself. I'm just the espresso. I'm just the shot in the morning to get you going to make you believe you can overcome that situation that you're dealing with all the time.[55]

In that moment, my entire view of Kanye West's brand was reframed.

His goal was to be the loudest, most egotistical person in the room, or even the world. While an incredibly successful career strategy, his approach had a direct impact on his fans' lives as well. Not only is Ye able to capture our attention through his personality and antics, but he also creates that

55 (BBC Radio 2017)

space for us all to be authentic, to be loud and assert our individuality.

And for that freedom, I thank Kanye West. But that's not all that Ye's self-love has to teach us.

Let's return to the example of the bachelor living in Rochester. Perhaps one of his real fans could choose to give him $3,000 one year, maybe even more, but that outcome is quite unlikely. However, he has one fan who can have that level of impact on his life every single year. His realest fan. Fan #1. No, not his mom, although we'll address that too. No, himself.

If that bachelor chooses to give up drinking alcohol to focus on his writing and swaps Friday nights at bars for sober nights playing cards with close friends, he can save money, avoid liver damage, skip many hungover mornings, and create more content and products. The example is not meant to condemn drinking alcohol (although it is literal poison).

You can make decisions that will enable you to achieve your dreams. You can view yourself as your most important fan. You can invest in your own work. You can love what you create.

You have partners in your life who will contribute in nonlinear ways as well. The people you date. Your roommate. A business partner. Your best friend. Your parents. Your mom might give you a jacket for your birthday. Your co-founder might give you advice that enables you two to grow your business's revenue and cover your cost of living. Your spouse might help you stay sane by being there to support you when you stretch yourself too thin.

As we've discussed throughout this book, your collaborators and partners will be critical to your success as a leader. Focus on building and maintaining relationships with your real-est fans rather than obsessing about how you'll get 500,000 followers on Twitter.

ACTION: Put this book down and call one of these friends, partners, or family members. If you can't call them, shoot them a text and ask if there's a time where you could meet up or video chat in the next week.

THE VIRTUE OF PESSIMISM

Pessimists assume that things will get worse, or not go according to plan, but they care about the outcome. They have an important function to play in challenging an overly optimistic consensus.

As a society, we need people to raise the alarm and ensure we're not lulled into a false sense of security. To solve complex problems, we need to hear different perspectives to best understand a given situation and how people feel about it.

My friend Muhammad Miqdad is the global operations manager at a company called PakVitae. Its mission is to expand access to drinking water throughout the developing world by implementing low-cost systems through collaborations with community stakeholders and NGOs. While Muhammad is driven by PakVitae's goal to provide access to more than 10 million people through their systems, he still identifies as a pessimist:

> When you grow up in a developing country, like Pakistan, or a country that has faced terrorism for a long time, you start to expect less and develop contingency plans in the back of your mind all the time.
>
> For example, growing up it was common that the power would go out randomly. When I would play video games, I would save my progress again and again because I knew that I might lose power and all my progress at any time.
>
> Pessimism is always hugging you, protecting you from unnecessary risks.

He brought this mentality with him to his work with PakVi-tae. For the past year, he has been managing a series of projects to implement the company's water-filtration systems throughout Africa. While his plan was to manage each of these projects directly by visiting each of the sites in-person, he feared that various issues would prevent him from following that plan.

"Right now, I had planned to be in Africa to help support our projects there," Muhammad explained. "When I started planning these projects, I recruited interns from all throughout Africa to help implement them. I hoped that I would be able to support the implementations in person, but I knew unforeseen difficulties could prevent me from getting there—maybe the payment will not be able to go through because of issues in the banking system, maybe the rupee will become devalued because of economic uncertainty. So I decided to train my interns under the assumption that I would be unable to carry out the plan and that they would need to be competent enough to execute it without my presence. Right now we're on Plan D, but everything is still moving forward successfully."

Muhammad's story demonstrates the merits of pessimism. The contingencies running through his head were critical to his mission. He found it stressful to overcome these obstacles, but his thorough planning and emphasis on training his interns prevented this challenge from turning into a catastrophe. Muhammad is a pessimist, but his perspective comes from his awareness that his actions will have a direct impact on the lives of others. While he cannot control the world, he can take responsibility for his actions.

Cynical nihilism is different from pessimism in this regard. It is a state of fatalism that finds its roots in despair. If you feel powerless to make an impact on the world, internalize that belief, and act (or don't act) with that in mind, it will become a self-fulfilling prophecy.

Whether you think you can, or you think you can't—you're right.

—HENRY FORD[56]

Those are my enemies: they want to overthrow and to construct nothing themselves. They say: "All that is worthless"—and want to create no value themselves.

—FRIEDRICH NIETZSCHE[57]

I am quoting Nietzsche, but I can speak from personal experience. My friends have felt this despair too. If you spend a

---

56   ("A Quote By Henry Ford" 2019)
57   ("Friedrich Nietzsche Quote" 2019)

lot of time on the internet, the world seems to have more problems than it has solutions or effective leaders. In some ways, that narrative may be true.

But I managed to overcome my nihilism when I realized I was despairing about problems that are, realistically, outside of my ability to significantly influence, let alone control.

Stephen Covey, author of *The Seven Habits of Highly Effective People*, posits a helpful model for thinking about our responsibilities and our ability to influence:

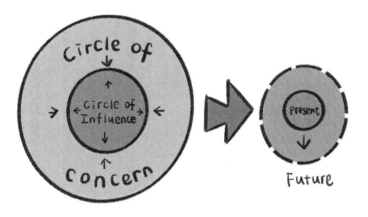

In Covey's model, we each have a circle of influence and circle of concern.[58] I have a relatively small circle of influence. No matter how concerned or busy I make myself, I probably

---

58 (Covey 2019)

could not decisively influence the result of anything related to, for example, U.S. national governance—let alone more complex problems that require buy-in from world leaders whose names I don't even know.

I could donate money to groups that promote the reforms or investments I'd like to see. I could start my own venture and, with great uncertainty, perhaps have a sizable impact on some sector of concern. My actions matter, but the relative magnitude of my influence is small. However, in the future, I plan to have a much greater circle of influence. Perhaps I might befriend individuals who have more influence and money. Or I'll become highly competent and experienced through years of deliberate training and hard work. Or I'll build international name recognition for writing a book that inspired others in consequential ways.

Each little way you can expand your influence—connections, brand reach, money, credibility, expertise, and character reputation—will expand your circle. Furthermore, I believe that your circle of concern should adjust to rise to the occasion. As Uncle Ben from *Spider-Man* said, "With great power comes great responsibility."

A tension exists in these ideas. I believe that our actions, regardless how small they seem, matter greatly because they have a compounding effect. I also believe that allowing yourself to be emotionally dependent on situations beyond your influence can be detrimental and even debilitating.

I reframe this idea in my own mind by choosing to believe that I can have the greatest circle of influence by focusing on problems that are sufficiently challenging, without becoming overwhelmed by the problems beyond my direct influence— Goldilocks problems.

We are not alone in this world, and we have people who share our values, who are much more competent, powerful, and influential. For me, training to be the most competent I can be in the long run is better than diverting too much of my energy toward problems that make me feel fatalistic. I choose to relate to the world this way because I find that this mindset enables me to stay healthy and maintain optimism about our future and my role in leading it. I am looking for Goldilocks problems, the ones that are just right for that time in my life.

Following the United States' decision to pull out of the Paris climate agreement, I became overwhelmed by feelings of existential dread. Conspiratorial thinking took over my brain, accompanied by feelings of hopelessness and cynical nihilism. I began to believe that the most powerful people in the United States did not in fact doubt climate science, but rather wholly accepted the most devastating predictions. Earth is a ticking time bomb, and they simply want to amass the resources necessary to ensure, through technology, their own family's survival.

I'd like to die on Mars, just not on impact.

—ELON MUSK, CEO OF SPACEX[59]

With the comparative clarity of mind that I have now, this idea seems preposterous. Life on Mars will be much less enjoyable than our life on Earth. While I hope that we become a spacefaring species, the first people to colonize another planet will be sacrificing their bodies, minds, and personal pleasure in an attempt to secure a prolonged future for humanity. My fatalistic thoughts were those of someone who was overwhelmed and delusional.

I had to take a step back, unplug, and develop this new model for living in the world. How would I be able to help influence the future if I was lying in bed depressed? Would those who are my ideological enemies not hope, or even plan, to try to shock and overwhelm me (indirectly)?

Millennials and Zoomers are the first generations to grow up in a world with near-global internet access, a massive communications network, and an endless stream of content.

---

59 (Terdiman 2013)

This territory is uncharted, and assumptions about the trajectory of our world are most likely going to be wrong. We will need to not only determine how to adapt to this new psychological environment, but also play a critical role in influencing its trajectory.

The bad news is that these feelings of despair and nihilism are propagating throughout our society, and they are causing severe damage, especially to youth. The reason why youth are becoming overwhelmed by such feelings of depression and anxiety is disputable, but you cannot credibly dispute that it's happening.

In the bestselling book *The Coddling of the American Mind* by Johnathan Haidt and Greg Lukianoff, the authors explore numerous potential reasons and share shocking statistics about the growing rates of self-harm among American youth:

> I took the average from federal data at the center for disease control. The rates for suicide were pretty stable in the early 2000s. For boys, the number who kill themselves each year was 11.9 per 100,000. This begins going up around 2010 to 2011, and by 2016–2017 the rate is 14.8 per 100,000 — an increase of 25%. Boys' suicide rate is up 25% which is huge. That is a lot of dead boys. That is a lot of tragedy.

For girls, it used to be 2.9 per 100,000 in the 2000s. Girls make more attempts at suicide, but they use reversible methods, so the girl rate is lower than the boys. For the last couple of years it has been 5 per 100,000 — so from 2.9 to 5. That's an increase of 70 percent. What do you think, is a 70% increase in suicide for teenage girls in this country an 'epidemic?'[60]

I think it is a tragedy and an epidemic. We each have a role to play in combating the factors driving young people to kill themselves, and many more to wallow in despair. Not only must we build a better future, but we need to model and promote a worldview which can overcome the bombardment of messages filling our world with fear, uncertainty, and doubt.

DEFINITE OPTIMISM

When I say that we need bold, inspirational plans for our future, I am saying that we need a global movement empowering more people to be definite optimists.

In his book *Zero to One*, Peter Thiel, Paypal co-founder and venture capitalist, outlined a four-quadrant model that

---

60 (Zadek 2018)

assessed societies as either definite or indefinite and optimistic or pessimistic. One of his goals in putting forth this idea was to encourage more people to develop concrete visions and take action to make them a reality.

To present a role model for definite optimism, Thiel shared the bold plan of John Reber:

> In the late 1940s, a Californian named John Reber set out to reinvent the physical geography of the whole San Francisco Bay Area. Reber was a school teacher, an amateur theater producer, and a self-taught engineer. Undaunted by his lack of credentials, he publicly proposed to build two huge dams in the Bay, construct massive freshwater lakes for drinking water and irrigation, and reclaim 20,000 acres of land for development. Even though he had no personal authority, people took the Reber Plan seriously. It was endorsed by newspaper editorial boards across California. The U.S. Congress held hearings on its feasibility. The Army Corps of Engineers even constructed a 1.5-acre scale model of the Bay in a cavernous Sausalito warehouse to simulate it. These tests revealed technical shortcomings, so the plan wasn't executed.

But would anybody today take such a vision
seriously in the first place?[61]

As someone who grew up during the period he describes as
indefinitely optimistic, I was amazed to hear this story. I can
imagine a powerful CEO, or a politician running for office,
proposing projects of such a significant magnitude, but not
a teacher. At least not in a way that would be taken seriously.

He defines the other three possibilities in his model:

> An indefinite pessimist looks out onto a bleak
> future, but he has no idea what to do about it...

> A definite pessimist believes the future can
> be known, but since it will be bleak, he must
> prepare for it...

> To an indefinite optimist, the future will be
> better, but he doesn't know how exactly, so
> he won't make any specific plans.[62]

Thiel's book was originally published in 2014. The world
has experienced quite a few shocks and changes since then.

---

61   (Thiel and Masters 2014)
62   (Thiel and Masters 2014)

Recognizing that this is not a science but a reductive model, I would argue that the world has become more definite since 2014.

Thiel had referenced China as his example of a society dominated by definite pessimism. He provocatively wrote, "From China's viewpoint, economic growth cannot come fast enough. Every other country is afraid that China is going to take over the world; China is the only country afraid that it won't."[63] China may still be pessimistic, but the Communist Party has ceded lifetime control to President Xi Jinping, giving him total power to enact a definite vision for the future. While they were definite before, President Xi must have presented a persuasive, hopeful vision to the other leaders in the Chinese Communist Party.

In 2014, Thiel had used the post-1982 United States as his example of an indefinitely optimistic society. While it's unclear if we've become more cynical about the future since 2014, we do seem to have transitioned toward being more definite. Political and business leaders are both proposing bold plans to fundamentally change the trajectory of our country and the world.

Democratic candidates for president are advocating transformational changes to our economic system in health care,

---

63 (Thiel and Masters 2014)

higher education, and energy. President Donald Trump ran and won on a differentiated, and divisive, vision for how he could "Make America Great Again." Elon Musk and Jeff Bezos are both leading companies to drastically reduce costs and expand our opportunities for space exploration. While many, or even all, of the aforementioned developments may make you pessimistic, please borrow my optimism for our future. The important point is that people are increasingly interested and open to bold, definite plans.

The indefinite world has awoken from its slumber, and people are again conscious of the idea that we must proactively identify problems and take deliberate action to solve them. In a definite world, the optimists have an advantage. We would all prefer to believe that our future will be brighter than it is today. In fact, that feeling of hope has enabled humanity to persist up until now. The only reason any of us are alive is because our ancestors decided to give birth to and raise children. They did this even while living lives of material deprivation, often coupled with the most brutal tragedies. Bubonic plague. Smallpox. Civil War. The Great War. The 1918 flu pandemic. World War II. Genocide. Many of the people you love and admire wouldn't be alive if their ancestors hadn't, despite their own personal experiences, believed in a brighter future for their children.

As leaders, we can seize this opportunity and choose to lead our friends, families, communities, and the world into a better future. We can identify problems, propose big and small solutions, and dedicate our energy, time, and attention to creating the future we know needs to exist. Human psychology is on our side, and we can ensure that we cultivate a world of competent, as opposed to naive, optimists.

The research of Israeli-American psychologist and 2002 Nobel Memorial Prize in economic sciences winner Daniel Kahneman reveals the advantage that optimists, especially the (over)confident, will have in leading our future:

> Overconfidence has many virtues. In the first place, it's nice, it's pleasant to be overconfident, especially if you're an optimist. Optimism is valuable, much more than overconfidence. Overconfidence is sort of a side effect. But to exaggerate the odds of success is a very useful thing for people. It will make them more appealing to others, they will get more resources, and they will take risks. It's not necessarily good for them. The expected utility of taking risks in the economy is probably moderately negative. But for society as a whole to have a lot of optimists taking risks — that's what makes for economic progress.[64]

---

64 (Cowen and Kahneman 2018)

Kahneman recognizes that most ideas are bad. Most new businesses fail. Most hypotheses are false. Individuals spend years of their lives trying to solve difficult problems, and most never achieve the success they strive for. Yet society improves, and each generation can have more opportunities than the last. Individuals take risks and sacrifice themselves in the pursuit of a better future. We lurch forward one failure at a time.

People have different experiences and personalities. I know not everyone will be optimistic about our future, and I wouldn't want to live in a world without pessimists. As demonstrated by Muhammad's story, pessimism has an important function in ensuring the success of any complex project. My hope in taking the time to discuss this model is to highlight the importance of making definite plans and taking concrete action to solve problems. We all have a role in combating the cynical nihilism overwhelming so many people. If we're going to have a better future, we need thoughtful, effective leaders to inspire others with compelling visions.

REFLECT: Which of these beliefs about our future do you think most accurately characterizes you? Are you surrounded by people who are optimistic or pessimistic? What about the media you consume—does it promote a positive vision of the future?

SKILL STACKS

The world has changed dramatically since I was born in 1994. Jobs exist that no one would have predicted. People play video games full time. People use computers to generate video that looks like a camera's recording. People make their own parody videos and memes and get paid by profitable companies for ad space. The coming decades will displace various jobs and create new opportunities that no one can predict.

Some jobs, of course, will likely exist throughout the entirety of our lives: doctor, computer programmer, hardware engineer, sales roles, and all sorts of entertainers. Even with that assumption, you have to mitigate the risk that you will end up unemployed or in a role that leaves you feeling unengaged and alienated.

As you attempt to plan for your future, you should consider a model at the intersections of the deterministic and probabilistic. The concept is that of the "skill stack."

As I mentioned earlier, and your experience would tell you, being the best person in the world at anything is difficult. Michael Phelps managed to become a swimming phenom and a household name, but that took an immense amount of resources, years of diligent training, and a series of rare genetic variations.[65] All of these needed to come together for him to become the best in the world. He was able to win the top tournaments to amass prestige and numerous, high-paying advertisement deals.

Unlike Phelps, or your preferred world-class performer in a field, most should try to develop a variety of complementary skills that will differentiate you from others, or your own skill stack.

I was first introduced to this idea when reading the blog of Derek Sivers, founder of CD Baby and prolific creator. I have heard a similar idea from other conventionally successful people—Tony Robbins, bestselling author and life coach, and Scott Adams, creator of the "Dilbert" comic strip, to name a few.

Derek calls them "multiplying skills":

> Learn the multiplying skills.
>
> Speaking, writing, psychology, design, conversation, 2nd language, persuasion, programming, meditation/focus.

---

65 (Parry 2008)

Not pursued on their own, they're skills that multiply the success of your main pursuit.

(A pilot who's also a great writer and public speaker.)[66]

Instead of focusing on becoming a master in one narrow field, you strive to become in the top 20 to 30 percent of a few distinct fields. You may not be the best writer, public speaker, computer programmer, or German conversationalist. But you could become one of the top ten people at the intersection of those skill sets. Then you can look for, or create, opportunities that will enable you to capitalize off your specific skill stack.

When I was growing up, my dad would often talk about his experience as a law student at The George Washington University. My dad is brilliant and hardworking; he graduated from SUNY Albany with a near flawless transcript. He had taken a significant amount of master's courses and paid his tuition by working overtime on a General Motors assembly line. He brought this same work ethic with him to GW. Since he was paying for all his classes and fascinated by the material, he "overloaded" again, continuing to take far more credits than required and confronting the most difficult courses head on.

---

66 (Sivers 2019)

When my dad graduated, his hard work paid off, and he landed a job as a tax lawyer at a prestigious New York City law firm. The people he interviewed with told him, "I just wanted to meet the guy who took all of those classes." However, my dad would not forget to mention that he did not get the best job, and neither did any of the particularly rich or privileged kids in his class. The person who got the best job was a woman whose family was German, who had learned how to speak conversationally while growing up.

She included her near-fluency on her resume when she applied for jobs. The firm that hired her was willing to offer her a ton of money and opportunities for advancement. Some of their biggest clients were German so they placed additional value on applicants who would be able to build rapport with them by speaking their mother tongue and be capable if they needed assistance with translations. Her skill stack enabled her to differentiate herself and made her the most valuable applicant in a specific context.

To further demonstrate how you might think about your own skill stack, here's how I am currently thinking about mine.

While I am willing to learn any skills necessary if I feel passionate about the opportunity, these are the skills I am focusing on:

- Marketing and sales
- Writing
- Conversation
- Additional languages—I aspire to become conversational in German, Mandarin, and Spanish
- Leadership and organizational design
- Public speaking

Once you have identified a set of skills you wish you to develop, you should develop systems that will enable you to regularly train each of them. You can do this by building habits and taking on projects that will require you to practice your skills. In chapter nine, we will explore methods for developing habits.

My understanding of my own skill stack influenced my decision to write this book.

The act of creating this book is helping me to train all these skills. To get people to read this book, I will need to experiment with different methods of marketing and convince people to buy it. The process of writing and receiving feedback from editors expanded my understanding of my strengths and weaknesses as a writer. Concretely articulating my ideas on a variety of topics will help me to communicate in conversation. While working on this book, I have spent time in China, Spain, and Germany, enabling me to practice my language skills. The additional research and reflection required to create this book has solidified any knowledge that I have on the topics of leadership and organizational design. And I hope to improve my public speaking by practicing on podcasts and radio shows and seeking paid speaking opportunities on the content of my book and blog posts.

While I would not claim to be in the top 70 to 80 percent of the world for any of those skills, I have systems and a framework to help me get there.

BRAINSTORM: Reflect on your own skill stack. What skills have you developed to a high level or do you seem to have a talent for? Are there skills you have an interest in that you think you should prioritize developing? Brainstorm a personal project that would allow you to develop these skills simultaneously.

In this chapter, we covered:

- Deterministic versus probabilistic models
- The bell curve
- Power laws
- 999 Real Fans
- Pessimism
- Definite optimism
- Skill Stacks

A deeper understanding of these ideas will take time to develop. Each of these frameworks is interesting alone, but combined they can help you improve your decision-making, identify opportunities, and increase your odds of becoming successful. I want all my readers to accelerate their personal and professional development. If we all strive to build and maintain valuable partnerships, develop competent skill stacks, and advance definitely optimistic plans for our future, we can have an extraordinary positive impact on the world.

CHAPTER 8

AMATEUR ECONOMICS

———

An understanding of the basic principles of economics is a useful tool for all leaders. In particular, I believe that the concepts of opportunity cost, sunk costs, and unintended consequences can help leaders improve the quality of their decisions by avoiding economic fallacies.

ACTION: Write a list of words you think of when you hear the term economics. (Hint: What do economists do? Why might someone choose to study economics in college? Try your best.)

Economic theory can be both unintuitive and powerful. I will briefly touch on a few basic concepts, but I would advise you to seek out at least one pop-economics book, such as *Economics in One Lesson* by Henry Hazlitt, or watch some introductory online lectures.

Feel free to ignore macroeconomic theory. While it has its uses, mainly for telling you what is improbable or impossible, it likely won't help you to make better decisions in your own life.

OPPORTUNITY COST

The first lesson is the idea of opportunity cost. Every decision you make has a cost associated with it. You have a finite amount of money, time, and other resources.

For example, if your friend invites you out to dinner on Friday but you already told your grandmother that you would take her to the movies at that time, you cannot choose to do both.

Economic theory would ask you to compare the costs and benefits of each of these options. In most examples, you have no way to compute which option would provide more "utility" and make a mathematically defined rational decision. Instead, when you decide to keep your word and take Omi to the movies, your choice demonstrates that you prefer that activity to eating dinner with your friend, given the circumstances. This is called a revealed preference.

Microeconomic theory relies on this type of analysis, where you are trying to maximize utility by comparing the costs and benefits of your options. These tools can be particularly useful in domains where the problem is well-defined mathematically. Unlike in the example with your grandma, you could use this to compare various financial products, such as the terms of different student loans or what credit card you should apply for, given your individual situation and preferences. Each decision comes with its associated trade-offs or opportunity costs.

SUNK COSTS

A sunk cost refers to an action or decision that you have already made and should be ignored when you make a future decision.

For example, you booked a bus to Krakow, Poland, from Warsaw. You spent $47 for the ticket and a three-night stay in a hostel in Krakow. However, on your last night in Warsaw, you approach one of the most beautiful people you have ever seen, chat with them briefly, and ask for their Instagram. They smile, share their handle with you, and immediately follow you back. Later on, you decide to direct message them and ask if they want to get an espresso the next day. They say, "YES!" Unfortunately, this coffee date means you will miss your bus and not use at least one of those nights at the hostel in Krakow.

When you make the decision to stay in Warsaw for at least one more day, you should not consider the cost of the ticket price or the hostel stay you have already paid for. You should consider the cost of purchasing another bus ticket and your additional night stay in Warsaw.

You should omit the costs that you have already realized (paid for), as these are the sunk costs. Whether you go to Krakow the next day or not, you have already spent the money and cannot get it back.

A simplistic version of this accounting might look something like this:

Benefits:

Item: Another day in Warsaw, Value: $X

Item: Espresso with the most beautiful person you've ever met, Value: $Y

Costs:

Item: Additional night's stay in Warsaw, Value: $10

Item: Two doppio espressos, Value: $5 [assuming you pay the bill]

Item: Additional bus ticket to Krakow, Value: $7

Item: Day not spent in Krakow, Value: $Z

Under microeconomic theory, your decision to stay would mean that you value: $\$X + \$Y > \$Z + \$10 + \$5 + \$7$.

However, if your date did not go well—they were late, rude, and picked their nose at the table—you would still be more likely to choose to go to Krakow on the next day because the cost of staying in Warsaw would involve you again paying for another hostel, while your hostel reservation in Krakow would still be waiting for you.

This example underpins that such decisions are full of unknowns and risks. Your optimism led you to deviate from your plan for the chance at love. It did not play out how you hoped, and perhaps your bank account regrets it, but that does not mean it was not a good decision. Based off the information and beliefs you had, it was a great decision. You are the only one who suffered for your actions and, had you ignored your heart (perhaps out of a misunderstanding of sunk costs), you might have regretted that decision even more. You cannot know otherwise.

UNINTENDED CONSEQUENCES

The third lesson is that of unintended consequences. The idea is that every decision will likely have effects that are not intended and were not at all considered at the time the decision was being made. Some of this may stem from the decision makers' inability to anticipate unintended consequences and others will be purely the result of randomness.

For example, in 1917, the United States was engulfed in a moral panic. The temperance movement gained sufficient influence to pass the Eighteenth Amendment to the Constitution. This amendment took effect January 16, 1920, and banned "the manufacture, sale, and transportation of alcoholic beverages in the United States and its possessions." While alcohol is a poison and its consumption is associated with violence and numerous health issues, people quite enjoy consuming it and wanted to purchase it regardless of its legal status.

The unintended consequences of the temperance movement and the Eighteenth Amendment were the proliferation of speakeasies—illicit establishments that sold alcohol—and significant increases in the price of alcohol, as its legal status deterred production and reduced supply. The high prices of alcohol encouraged mobsters to develop local monopolies over the sale of alcohol, as it was immensely profitable. This development encouraged gang violence as rival groups fought to maintain their monopoly power. The most infamous mobster of the Prohibition era may be Al Capone, a dominant bootlegger in Chicago.

Furthermore, without the Eighteenth Amendment, the characters and movies inspired by Al Capone would never have been created—classics such as *Scarface, Capone,* or *The Untouchables,* to name a few. The temperance movement's leaders were not thinking about Sean Connery's acting career when they were lobbying politicians to pass the Eighteenth Amendment.

Every competent legislative body now needs to consider the unintended consequences of directly banning any prized commodity. After deliberation, they may decide that any resulting black markets are worth the benefits provided by the ban, but they must acknowledge the creation of a black market and its consequences.

This understanding of unintended consequences influenced Portugal's decision to decriminalize usage of illicit drugs in 2001, in favor of a policy focused on harm reduction. While this system is complex, with many variables, the results are resonant with economic theory and positive in a way that demands other states analyze the data that has been generated since Portugal's policy change.

Since Portugal decriminalized the use of all illicit drugs— opioids, marijuana, cocaine, etc.—the country has seen a dramatic reduction in HIV transmission due to drug usage. In 2000, drug users accounted for 52 percent of new HIV and

AIDS diagnoses in Portugal, or 1,430 out of 2,758 cases. In 2015, transmission resulting from drug use accounted for a low of 6 percent of all new diagnoses, or 77 out of 1,228 cases.[67]

Especially considering the devastation caused by the opioid crisis in the United States, the reduction in overdose deaths is even more amazing. More than 72,000 Americans died due to overdose in 2017.[68] If the United States had the same rates of overdose-related death as Portugal, around three per million, the United States would have instead only seen approximately 1,000 overdose-related deaths.[69] While we cannot attempt to make a direct comparison between these two situations, the sheer potential for reduction in lives, families, and communities destroyed demands further investigation and consideration.

The temperance movement example is more related to our earlier discussion about complexity. If you had a personal temperance movement, imposed one on your household, or even convinced your village to participate, the effort would not have had the same magnitude of unintended consequences. We must always consider at which scale we should solve problems. The temperance movement might have had

---

67 (*Drug Decriminalization In Portugal: A Health-Centered Approach* 2015)
68 ("Vital Statistics Rapid Release - Provisional Drug Overdose Data" 2018)
69 (Ingraham 2015)

more sustained success had it only focused on winning over individuals, families, and communities. On the other hand, we wouldn't have all these Al Capone movies.

TIP THE WAITSTAFF

Let us again consider the idea of cost-benefit analysis. People with less-developed empathy and intuition commonly begin applying the concept in ways that are socially and personally detrimental. They may begin to use this concept to rationalize not paying their fair share, or acting as a "free rider."

For example, our recent Economics 101 graduate Brad may be invited to Susan's barbecue. As Brad decides whether to attend, he now begins to think about the occasion as an opportunity to maximize utility (increase benefits, lower costs). Based off his naive economic understanding, he believes that he will be the "best off" if he does not reciprocate by bringing a large apple pie and a jug of lemonade, as not providing anything will decrease his costs. He may bring only a quantity that could not be shared, or even choose to free ride, bringing nothing and truly "maximizing utility."

This approach is intuitively not a good way for Brad to think about Susan's barbecue.

First off, he may have a much better time if he brings the large apple pie because the other partygoers will tell him how good it was and use that as an opportunity to start a deeper conversation with him.

Second, Susan chose to invite him to her party when she had no obligation to. She clearly values his friendship and knowing she doesn't need to worry about providing dessert will make her happy (as it is appropriate to let the host know what you will be bringing ahead of time).

Less intuitively, perhaps, Brad did not consider that Susan, or the other attendees, may notice that he ate as many ribs as possible during the festivity but arrived empty-handed. That when the party runs out of lemonade, the others may think, *I wish we had more*, and remember that Brad contributed nothing.

In this next example, Brad is interacting with strangers.

Brad goes to an American diner alone one morning because he has a craving for pancakes and bacon. After struggling to find a girlfriend, he is about to move to a larger city, believing that a larger population will help solve his problem.

The waitress, Olga, smiled when she spoke and ensured his coffee cup was perpetually full. However, when the time to pay the bill came, Brad chose to only leave sweet Olga $1, a 10 percent tip. Brad rationalized that he would never see her again, and by keeping that extra dollar, he had profited, or even "won."

This time, I'll spare you the story of how one day, Olga turns out to be the cousin of the first girl he seriously dates in the larger city and takes it upon herself to sabotage their relationship (although stranger things have happened!). No, our antihero does not directly feel the negative consequences of his decision to tip Olga only $1. Instead, he experiences satisfaction for employing his great economic thinking. He proceeds to continue this behavior of viewing every tipping decision as a contest between him and the service staff.

In the larger city, he finds even more opportunities to view scenarios as ones where he will never have to see someone again. Brad does begin to tip less when he goes out with friends and they get separate checks. His friends begin to notice. They do not confront him, but they begin to see this attitude playing out in other aspects of his life. Soon after, our antihero begins to feel alienated as his friends "forget" to invite him to outings and are "tired" when he invites them to hang out.

Viewing your relationships the way poor Brad has viewed his entails a number of problems. To name two:

First, humans are habit-forming creatures, so you likely can't avoid expanding the interpersonal scenarios in which you would misapply this economic framework.

Second, the people around you may notice and they will empathize with the people you are treating this way.

In game theory, a game refers to an instance of an interaction between two or more players; each player has options to choose from and each set of responses has a payout, or expected utility, for each player. Economists use this type of model to determine what types of behavior are likely to emerge given each player's incentives and understanding of one another's preferences.

The world should not be modeled as a bunch of one-off games, but rather as a series of repeating games. In game theory, and in the customs of my grandmothers, you should almost always tip at least 20 percent in the United States and view your relationships with your friends, and most strangers, as win-win. Treating others with dignity and respect is the best life strategy.

When our antihero was deciding to only tip Olga $1, his justification was based on the assumption that he was playing an independent, one-off game. He believed that he would never see her again, and if he did, she wouldn't recognize him or remember. What our antihero did not consider is that to any outside observer there is no difference between a one-off game and the last game.

When his friends noticed his behavior, they unconsciously began to wonder when this behavior would harm them or their loved ones. They intuitively realized that if their friend had no problem cheating waitstaff because he viewed that relationship as expendable, at some point he may view their relationship similarly. Perhaps he would lose a bet and refuse to pay. Or they would ask him for help when they fell upon hard times and he would ignore them. Such outcomes may not necessarily happen, but this line of thinking is the reasonable, intuitive response when someone notices this pattern of behavior in another.

If you think you can shirk social convention because of an economic or psychological theory, I would encourage you to be a bit more skeptical. While there are antiquated social customs, the ones that exist to encourage people to treat others with dignity and respect exist for a reason. Ignore them at your own peril. The consequences of those actions are likely to catch up to you. Listen to your grandparents or, if you don't have any, consider adopting some at a local church or retirement home.

This mental model for understanding the world will best enable you to avoid making antisocial decisions that will unintentionally harm you and others in the future. As we've discussed throughout this book, if you want to lead others effectively, you must develop partnerships and methods for building and maintaining relationships. Like our antihero, you will be unable to contain the negative effects generated by acting in antisocial ways. Instead of naively seeking to maximize short-term "utility," a deeper understanding of economic theory and leadership would suggest that you try to use each interaction as an opportunity to think win-win, develop your social skills, and cultivate a way of living that improves the lives of others.

I would encourage you to further consider:

- Opportunity costs
- Sunk costs
- Unintended consequences
- Why you should interact with strangers and friends as if you will continue to interact with them for the rest of your life

A deep understanding of these basic concepts will change your day-to-day decision-making. They can help you avoid making poor decisions by giving you a tool kit to reframe and analyze problems. This understanding will become more critical as your leadership career accelerates and the consequences of bad decisions become larger, not only for you but also for those who are impacted.

CHAPTER 9

80/20 HABITS OF HIGHLY EFFECTIVE LEADERS

———

"80/20" in the title of this chapter refers to another version of the power law, known as the Pareto principle. The idea is to examine what 20 percent of behaviors are responsible for 80 percent of results. As we have explored before, there may even be a 5 percent of all behavior responsible for 50 percent of the results.

My hope with this chapter is to outline a model for thinking about our routines and simple ways for building, removing, or replacing existing habits.

While writing and editing this book, I was on an adventure throughout China and Europe. I spent the night in over twenty different locations. The amount of change in my environment was chaotic and extremely fun. New places, people, and experiences occupied part of every day.

However, even during a short stay in a city, I began to fall into habits. I went to the same cafe near my hostel every morning for my coffee. I bought my bottle of water at the same supermarket. Or decided to avoid public transportation and walked everywhere instead.

For most of my trip, I was traveling alone. I found the times I was solo-traveling to be more exhausting than when I was accompanied by friends. I believe there are two main reasons for this:

First, every decision was my responsibility. I could not decide to just follow a friend's preferences and enjoy the ride. I had to decide what sites I was going to visit, when I was going to work, where I was going to eat, and any of the other hundreds of decisions I was confronted with every day.

Second, since I was traveling alone, I needed to be extra aware of my surroundings. While most people would be willing to help me if there was an emergency, it was best to put in the effort to evade any crises. I devoted a lot of my attention to avoiding forgetting anything or getting pick pocketed.

MAKING CONSCIOUS DECISIONS

Consciously making decisions is tiring. People develop routines to simplify their lives, or at least reduce the number of decisions they need to make. This process can be conscious or unconscious, but everyone develops lifestyle patterns, even if they're only temporary.

Perhaps most famously, Mark Zuckerberg is focused on minimizing the amount of decisions that he makes:

> I'm in this really lucky position, where I get to wake up every day and help serve more than a billion people. And I feel like I'm not doing my job if I spend any of my energy on things that are silly or frivolous about my life.[70]

Zuckerberg received a lot of press for his decision to wear the same outfit every day. He removed the other clothing options, so he never needed to think about it. When he wakes up in the morning, he simply puts on that day's gray t-shirt without a second thought.

---

70   (Saul 2016)

I am not suggesting you follow Zuckerberg's example. Personally, I like to wear different outfits every day (although I hate shopping). My hope in bringing this case to your attention is to provoke a more thorough reflection about the patterns of behavior you default to and how habit formation can become a powerful tool to help you achieve your goals.

In his interview with Tim Ferriss, Jim Collins, business consultant and bestselling author of *Build to Last*, described what he calls his "bug book."[71] The name is a reference to the type of observation research you may have done when you first learned about the scientific method in school. In his bug book, he describes his own behavior in a descriptive way.

An entry might be as simple as:

- Grant eats pizza faster than he eats other foods.
- Grant drinks an Americano every morning.
- Grant seems relaxed after a long walk.
- Grant has more energy after a long conversation with a friend.

Collins recommends keeping a pocket-sized notebook ready in which you can casually log these observations. This practice will give you insights into habits you have that you are

---

71 (Ferriss and Collins 2019)

not consciously aware of. As I will touch on later, intentional journaling and introspection are similar tools for better understanding yourself.

There's a cue, which is like a trigger for the behavior to start unfolding. There's a routine, which is the habit itself, the behavior, the automatic sort of doing what you do...And then, at the end, there's a reward. And the reward is how our neurology learns to encode this pattern for the future.

And most people, when they think about habits, they focus on the behavior or the routine. But what we've learned is that it's the cue and the reward that really determine why a habit unfolds.

—CHARLES DUHIGG, THE POWER OF HABIT[72]

REFLECT: What are some of your habits? Make a list. Which are affecting your life positively, and which negatively?

You have no choice in whether you will have habits. Even a conscious practice to willfully be spontaneous and shirk routine would involve behavior that could be considered a habit. I believe such an extreme is not possible, but I do believe people have some power to choose and cultivate their routines.

72　(Fox and Duhigg 2012)

Numerous books have been written about habits, even in the last decade. People keep writing them and other people keep buying them. Personally, I read *Triggers* by Dr. Marshall Goldsmith.

Feel free to read all of the books on the subject, but here's the short of it:

- Habits get reinforced the more you do them; any new behavior not done for a minimum of eighteen days is not a habit.[73]

- These conscious choices take energy, so it is best to focus on building one (or two) habits at a time.[74]

- No shortcuts exist.

- Habits are triggered by cues in our environment; altering your environment can be a powerful tool when building new habits or replacing existing ones.

- Associate a reward with a new habit—i.e., end a meditation session by writing down three things you're grateful for or drink a tasty protein shake after your workout.[75]

---

73 (Lally et al. 2009)
74 (Danziger, Levav and Avnaim-Pesso 2011)
75 (Fox and Duhigg 2012)

If you can internalize and act on those principles, you can alter and add habits. Developing a specific habit may not be easy, but it is that simple. Figuring out how to add new habits or, more importantly, replace bad habits is a critical skill.

ACTION: Think about the habits you wrote earlier. How will you use these principles to change bad habits or build new ones?

During my time at iZone, I became determined to again attempt to build habits that would enable me to cope with stress and operate at a high level. I started my first day of work by going to the gym, opening a locker, and recording my starting weights for each lift in a note on my phone. I ended that first session by eating a tasty breakfast sandwich and drinking coffee in the sunshine.

My ideal routine was to wake up with enough time to exercise and eat breakfast before I needed to be at work every single day. I struggled most days to act out that ideal. As time went on, I found that I needed to improve other aspects of my lifestyle to overcome my desire to stay in bed. Exercise was the domino that pushed me to make those other lifestyle changes. Once I truly made exercise a habit, I felt healthier than I have in my entire life. I began to sleep eight hours a night, eat well, and floss every day.

At the end of my first year of work, I decided to move into a studio apartment. This change in environment and next level of autonomy created the perfect environment to expand on these habits. My old room had psychological baggage. My bed was associated with ignoring my alarm, snoozing it, and staying in bed until the fear of being late pushed me into the shower. My couch was associated with getting home from work and feeling like lying around listening to podcasts and watching Netflix.

Once I entered my new apartment, I used that as an opportunity to only create the associations that I wanted. My bed was associated with sleeping and getting up when my alarm went off. My wooden chair was associated with writing in my journal. My computer chair was associated with playing video games or hanging out. My room was associated with this version of myself that had a series of habits to work on every day and did them faithfully.

You can find many easier ways to change your associations with your environment. They might be as simple as finding a way to alter the smell of your room, rearranging your furniture, or removing items you don't need anymore. My goal in sharing this story is to encourage you to use every new environment as an opportunity to build new associations. Your first associations in a new space are important.

ALWAYS BE TRAINING

When I return from my adventure and seek to build new routines, I will start by rebuilding my exercise habit. From my experience, it is the one habit that most enables the others.

Quick reasons to exercise:

- Exercise seems to play a role in regulating our brain chemistry.[76]

- Exercise reduces your risk of health issues related to your cardiovascular system.[77]

- Exercise may improve your ability to make decisions and perform academically.[78]

- People who exercise often have higher energy than those who do not.

- It encourages other behaviors that will enable you to be healthy.

Beyond any of those reasons, or what the psychological research may tell us, my assumption would be that stressing

---

76 (Heijnen et al. 2016)
77 (Myers 2003)
78 (Tomporowski et al. 2007)

our bodies through exercise is critical to what it means to be human. Before the agricultural revolution, humans were hunters and gatherers. Just because all we need to do to access food is open the Grubhub app and meet the delivery person at the door doesn't mean that our body doesn't desire the exercise that would have preceded any of our ancestors' feasts.

When humans have captured other predators and put them into unnatural environments, they have struggled to survive or suffered from unanticipated problems. For example, when the Seneca Park Zoo in Rochester added a polar bear exhibit, the polar bear began to pace back and forth, spending up to a third of its day walking in a distinct pattern. By spending millions of dollars to try to create an environment and activities that were more comparable to its natural habitat, the zoo was able to reduce that pacing behavior by half.[79]

If polar bears start to exhibit unnatural behavior due to their placement in an unnatural habitat, why would our assumption be that humans would not as well? We all accept that we need sunlight to be healthy; why would we assume we don't need exercise?

---

79 (Yates 2003)

Exercise is a rabbit hole of a topic to explore. If you develop the habit, you will fall down the hole, but it's up to you how far you fall.

Whatever you do, don't let the "need" for more research become an excuse to not get started.

Here are three steps to get started, for those who have not had the habit before:

- Google "beginner workout <type of exercise (running, weight training, etc)>" or simply look into "weight-lifting 5x5 strong lifts."

- Find a public park or gym that will be convenient for your schedule, and make sure it has any basic equipment that you need.

- Start easy and focus first on building the habit—the actual benefits in performance will come from consistent training.

One trap people fall into around their exercise habit is to view it as a to-do or a chore. This framing turns it into a burden rather than an opportunity to invest in yourself and your future. If you have momentum and are deep in the habit, this framing is fine, but it won't help you when life works to disrupt your routine.

My friend, Vita Benes, founder of deprocrastination.co, introduced me to the idea of reframing my exercise routine as a form of training:

> Reframing has powerful personal applications.
>
> Exercise is training to become stronger for life. Meditation is finding silence to train your awareness. Taking a cold shower is training your ability to push through discomfort.[80]

By viewing exercise as a form of training, it becomes an opportunity to invest in yourself. Exercise is not a chore to check off your to-do list, but rather a direct and clear way to expand your own future potential.

Starting with exercise is powerful because it has feedback mechanisms to reward you for your efforts. As I mentioned above, it will help you regulate your brain chemistry and give you more energy. You will clearly see progress as you continue or restart your workout habit. If you track your performance, eat the right food, and sleep enough, the results

---

80 (Benes 2019)

of your training will be empowering. Not only will you be aware of the changes to your body and your mind, but others will take notice as well.

THE HYDRATION EQUATION

If you commit to your training, you will need to drink more water. If you are not properly hydrated, you will become too fatigued to keep your routine and risk hurting yourself.

This section doesn't need to be long because it's simple, yet important:

- Get a water bottle that you like—I bought a metal water bottle off Amazon in 2016 and I still use it daily.

- Fill and drink from it.

    - People disagree about how much water you need to drink, as it will vary from person to person—aim for two liters a day and be sure to drink when you feel thirsty.

- Don't lose it!

Seventy-five percent of the human brain is composed of water. If you don't drink enough water, you will become dehydrated and your ability to make decisions may be affected.[81]

If water is readily accessible, or you know that it may be difficult to access, you have no excuse for not staying hydrated. If you are taking responsibility for others, this habit is simple for improving your thinking and maintaining your energy.

SLEEP...THE COUSIN OF DEATH?

Inhale deep like the words of my breath

I never sleep, 'cause sleep is the cousin of death

I lay puzzled as I backtrack to earlier times

Nothing's equivalent to the New York state of mind

—NAS, N.Y. STATE OF MIND

After multiple years of excellent sleep, I don't know how my body survived when I was in high school. Most weekdays I slept fewer than six hours per night. This topic, like anything relating to the body, varies from person to person, but here's the gist.

---

81   (Patsalos and Thoma 2019)

A few reasons why sleep is important:

- Sleep is critical to learning and memory formation.

- Sleep enhances your problem-solving skills, improves your attention, and enables you to make better decisions.

- Sleep deficiency has been linked to depression and greater risk of suicide.

- Sleep deficiency may increase your risk of heart disease, kidney disease, high blood pressure, diabetes, and stroke.

- Sleep deficiency weakens your immune system, leaving you more susceptible to illness.[82]

Beyond the research, you will experience the importance of sufficient sleep if you commit to your training. Anyone who has developed an exercise routine is personally aware of the impact on your recovery and performance. If you think there needs to be a complicated argument, try to set a new personal record on three hours of sleep (NOTE: not an actual recommendation).

---

82   (Krause et al. 2017)

This list is by no means a full account of the reasons why sleep is important. If you're still reading at this point, I'm going to assume that those effects are compelling.

Many days throughout the past year, I would fail to get to bed early enough to get eight hours of sleep before my alarm would go off. On the days when I dragged myself to the gym, I would always have a lackluster performance. When I was eating breakfast after my workout, I was always glad I got out of bed. I was seldom able to complete my sets, let alone set a new personal record.

When you are under a lot of stress, you become vulnerable as your immune system is weakened. To make the best decisions and show up to work, training, and your other commitments every day, you need to get your rest.[83]

Key advice for better sleep:

- Stop looking at digital screens at least an hour before bed.

- Use f.lux or put your phone in monochrome (black and white only) to remove the blue spectrum light which stimulates your brain.[84]

---

83 (Krause et al. 2017)
84 ("Research Progress About The Effect And Prevention Of Blue Light On Eyes" 2018)

- Only use your bed for sleep.

- Stop consuming caffeine at least ten hours before you want to be asleep, or quit it altogether.

- Consider getting a non-phone alarm—preferably one that does not project light into your room.

- Explore options to reduce light: blinds, sleep mask, or other ways to cover any light entering your room. It is helpful for your room to be as dark as possible.[85]

- Wake up and go to sleep at the same times every day, even if you don't have the same daily commitments.

- Wake up early, exercise, and make the most of every day.

I have many days when I fall right to sleep, even though I spent most of my day relaxing and being unproductive. However, I have never had a day when I worked out, was productive on work or personal projects, did not abuse caffeine in the afternoon, and did not collapse into bed exhausted.

When I would tell my coworkers that I was working out before work, they thought I was a "morning person" and a

---

85 (Stenvers et al. 2016)

bit crazy. But I have never been a morning person, and that had nothing to do with it. I spent every night of my youth staying up late on the computer and the following day either sleep-deprived or sleeping past noon.

My newfound ability to start my day with a powerful routine was unrelated to the type of person I am. I simply decided that I wanted to do it and took the steps to make it happen. Saying, "I couldn't do that; I'm a night owl" is just a reason to justify why you are not doing it. If you do not want to work out in the morning, that is reasonable. I even believe it's likely that some people are better at waking up early than others. However, if you think developing that habit aligns with your vision for yourself, you should not create barriers through this type of self-justification. You have the power to do it, if you want to.

As I have said, my ideal self goes to sleep for eight hours a night, wakes up before 6 a.m., and starts every day with exercise. Doing so is seldom glorious. I am cranky while I walk to the gym and bombarded by negative thoughts. I have a bad workout. I have to say no to watching another episode of Netflix, or tell my friends that I need to go home at 8:30 p.m. But when you are on the other side of that morning workout (showered, well-fed, and perhaps calm after some good meditation), you will feel content and powerful.

This approach is not a set of tasks to check off your checklist because "that's what my preferred influencer does." No. It's a challenge to overcome and an opportunity to alter how you view yourself. You can become someone who can wake up early in the morning. You can become someone who has the discipline to follow through even when their brain is telling them to go back to bed. These are not difficult. You are capable of overcoming much more difficult challenges.

LISTEN TO YOUR BODY

If exercise information is a rabbit hole, then diet is a tunnel to the center of the earth.

What you eat matters. It impacts our ecology, economy, health care costs, life expectancy (which has declined in the United States in the last three years[86]), and many more aspects of our world. For many, deciding what to eat is not only a decision about their health but also a moral question. If you are conscious about your food choices, you will recognize that they affect you in surprising and consequential ways.

If you want to be operating at your best, cereal for breakfast and pizza for lunch is not going to get you there.

---

86 ("Mortality In The United States, 2017" 2018)

Throughout my time in high school, cereal and pizza were staples of my diet. If I had enough energy to eat breakfast before going to school, I would eat cereal. If I didn't have enough energy, I would eat a sugar-rich muffin from the school cafeteria.

I never packed a lunch from home and would instead eat the school cafeteria food every day. That usually meant: a burger, a spicy chicken sandwich, a ham and cheese wrap, or pizza. It mostly meant pizza. I would eat an iceberg lettuce salad drenched in ranch, chocolate milk, and a chocolate chip cookie to chase it down.

After school, I would often eat pizza with my best friend, Nick, or eat cereal at home. If I was out getting pizza, I would also order a soda or grab an energy drink from the local Sunoco. Knowing what I know now, I am surprised I was as functional as I was. Almost every meal my parents didn't cook for me consisted of sugar, carbs, a little bit of protein or fat.

When I arrived at college, I began to think more about my dietary choices and how they were impacting my life. On the first day of college, my new friends and I went to the dining hall together. What happened next would change my life.

We set our college IDs down on the table and went to go grab food from the buffets. I went to the soda fountain and filled my glass with Mountain Dew and set it on the table. I continued foraging from the dining hall and grabbed a burger and a plate of barbecue chicken and rice. As I sat down at the table, my friend Sam said, "Dude, you drink soda? That's disgusting! I only drink water and coffee."

As I mentioned earlier, I was an impressionable freshman, and after facing my new friend Sam's judgment, I never drank soda in the dining hall again and have purchased it only a dozen or so times since. I did my own research. Sam was right: drinking soda every day was not going to do me any favors.

If you want to achieve a higher level of personal performance, you are going to need a nutritious diet tailored to what works for your body.

DISCLAIMER: I am not a doctor and never will be.

But here's the short of it:

- Limit consumption of processed sugar, or even cut it out of your life.

- Prefer simple, whole foods that your great, great grandparents would have eaten: vegetables, meat, and some fruit.

- Simplicity. The only diet that matters is the one you can sustain—you need to build systems that will enable you to follow through on your plan for yourself.

- Nothing about human anatomy demands you eat three meals a day—brief periods of fasting, say sixteen to twenty hours, may be either neutral or positive for your physical health.[87]

People become obsessed with their diet. In 2019, an incredible amount of food choices are available. Even five years ago, many dietary preferences—vegan, vegetarian, and gluten-free options, to name a few—were far less available. Now the supply has matched a new demand and it's more a matter of your budget, the choices you make when you go shopping or go to a restaurant, and your ability to adopt habits that enable you to sustain your diet.

Personally, I found that following a "Slow Carb Diet," as popularized in Tim Ferris' *The Four Hour Body*, worked great for me. I did not feel like I was sacrificing too many of my favorite foods, my energy was great, and it enabled me to perform at a high level when training. It also enabled me to have a six-pack for the first time since I grew into my lanky, post-growth-spurt body.

---

87 (Wilhelmi de Toledo et al. 2019)

In order to succeed in this diet, I needed a simple system:

- Develop a habit of saying no to processed grains and sugar by committing to it for two weeks.

- Start the day by eating eggs and black coffee—this technique helped me avoid hunger because of the high fat content and caffeine.

- Prepare small meals to bring to work or school by cooking a batch of chicken, sausage, vegetables, or soup at the beginning of the week.

- Identify a few restaurants that have dishes you enjoy that meet your restrictions—places you would recommend if you were making plans to meet a friend out for a meal.

- Figure out a few simple meals you enjoy and can default to—I would cook a stir fry with a mix of vegetables, eggs, and meat.

You will need to figure out what works for you, but the point is to figure out a simple system that will enable you to succeed. Focus on simplifying, and then build a habit around it.

And, if you stray from your system, forgive yourself and try again!

I have not personally engaged in a ton of analysis of primary research on diet and nutrition. The field is full of contradictory claims and information, and even the scientists who work in the field find it challenging. The human body is one of the most complex systems to have ever existed. What might work for me, or the average person, might be terrible for you.

Be sure to always consult professionals and do your own thorough, independent research before doing anything extreme. Likewise, be aware of changes in your energy and any pain or lack of pain that comes when you start restricting specific foods from your diet.

For example, I started bringing cheese to work as part of my lunch and realized that it made me sleepy and low-energy. After this realization, I decided to stop bringing cheese for lunch and to switch from a whey protein powder to a brown rice protein powder for my pre-workout shake. Both these changes created a noticeable improvement in my energy in the morning and afternoon.

You will need to experiment and determine what works for you. Research will at least give you some insight into common problems and an incomplete but useful model for thinking about nutrition.

WRITE IT JUST TO SEE HOW IT FEELS

Know thyself.

—ATTRIBUTED TO NUMEROUS GREEK SAGES (HERACLITUS, PYTHAGORA, SOCRATES, THALES OF MILETUS)

One of the most powerful habits I have ever developed is a consistent journaling practice. As I have mentioned throughout this book, writing is a powerful tool for reflecting on your life, processing information, and planning your future. If you have not written a single word since you started reading this book, stop reading now and go find a journal to write a couple sentences in. Let today be the first day of your practice.

My own journaling practice started in Hong Kong, after my senior year at university had left me feeling burnt out. I had been given a blue moleskine journal as a gift to document my adventures abroad. After a few weeks into my adventure, I had not written a single word.

On that day, I was distressed by terrible news from the United States—the 2016 mass shooting in Dallas, Texas. I was browsing social media, and I felt lonely being away from my communities after a national tragedy. For whatever reason, these emotions pushed me over the edge and I recognized that I needed to open my journal and write to process everything on my mind. Subconsciously, I had been preoccupying myself with podcasts, social media, and my studies to distract myself from the need to look inward.

This was not the first time that I had purchased a journal and carried it with me for weeks without using it. I had a mental block where I felt I needed something significant to say before it was worth writing at all. So, I did what I think many newbie journalers do—in my emotional state, I decided to write about why I hadn't been writing and how that was nonsense.

I started my journal by writing:

> This journal is worthless. It has absolutely no value. No one is going to buy it from me and I'm not interested in selling it. It is my journal and I can fill it full of any nonsense that I want to. I could write the same sentence again and again and that would be fine…

After two pages of this private diatribe, my mental block was broken. I started writing about the events that had pushed me into this emotional state. From then on, I wrote a little every day and sought to make a habit out of it. I have not managed to write every single day since then, but I have managed to fill close to two notebooks every single year. When I lose my habit, I forgive myself and pick it back up.

How to start a journaling practice:

- Get a journal. All you need is paper and preferably some way to keep it together—feel free to repurpose an old school notebook.

- Find a pen you like to write with.

- Write the date, and then write about whatever you want. I've included some prompts below, but you can also just think of it as a free-association, stream-of-consciousness exercise. Writing the first sentence is enough to get yourself going:

  - What makes you angry?

  - Why do you want to journal?

  - What stupid things are you doing in your life?

  - What are you grateful for?

  - When was the last time you hung out with your best friend?

  - The last time you spent time one on one with your mom?

If you do this every day until it feels weird to miss, you'll have a journaling practice.

Like the other habits, it's simple—but that doesn't mean it's easy. You may avoid writing about topics that you want to think through. When you have been suppressing your own thinking by consuming the content of others, you might be afraid of what will come from your pen. The easiest way to get started is to write garbage and nonsense until you decide it would be less painful to just write about what you're afraid of.

I recommend this practice because it has helped me in a number of ways:

- Our ability to remember, and mine especially, is much worse than we like to believe; having written documentation of my thoughts and reasoning allows me to see the changes in my thinking over time.

- If you write about what makes you angry or upset, you will be forced to articulate the problems that you have in your life; identifying a problem is critical to figuring out how to solve it.

- Writing is therapeutic; it helps me to get ideas out of my head that otherwise might keep my mind running when I want to fall asleep.

- Technology has made consuming content and ideas easier and easier, but it has done little to encourage people to think for themselves; creating space to think is vital to processing the information you're consuming and figuring out how to apply it.

- Many people write publicly on the internet, but in public most people feel pressure to cater to their audience; writing for yourself creates a different dynamic and will give you insight into how you may be influenced by peer pressure.

These bullets are only scratching the surface of my own experience, and yours might be completely different. You may have different takeaways from your journaling practice depending on how you use it, but I guarantee if you spend even ten minutes a day journaling, you will develop a greater understanding of yourself.

I LIKE BIG BOOKS

A reader lives a thousand lives before he dies. The man who never reads lives only one.

—GEORGE R. R. MARTIN, *A DANCE WITH DRAGONS*[88]

---

88 ("A Quote From A Dance With Dragons" 2019)

One of the habits I have been committed to that most stands out to my peers is the amount of time I spend reading. According to Pew Research, "Americans read an average (mean) of 12 books per year, while the typical (median) American has read 4 books in the last 12 months."[89] Hopefully you'll end up reading more books than the typical American this year.

I don't think I need to convince you of why reading is a good idea. Instead, I'd like to give you a few recommendations to consider:

- Read old books, as they are more likely to challenge your assumptions.

- Read books no one is talking about.

- Choose to read the books your school tried to force you to read (I did end up reading *To Kill A Mockingbird* after falling asleep in English class, by the way. 10/10, would recommend).

- Read books written by people you disagree with—don't forget that you can check them out of the library.

- Use your local library!

- Read fiction. It often has more to teach us than nonfiction.

---

89 (Perrin 2016)

- Rereading books is often even more worthwhile than reading a new book—the book may stay the same, but we don't.

- Read before bed, before work or school, and during your lunch break.

- Read on your phone in place of scrolling through social media.

- Read whatever interests you enough to read every day.

Reading is a personal experience and should be viewed as a hobby and not a chore. You can read whatever and however you want. Check a book out of the library and only read one chapter that's interesting to you. Start reading a book and know it's okay to put it down and move on if it's not engaging you. Buy a used book and feel free to underline, write in the margins, or fill it full of sticky notes. Avoid telling yourself that you need to read anything because of someone else's recommendation, or that it's a waste of your time to read fiction that keeps you turning the pages. You reserve the right to pick things up and put them down, to skim the surface or dive in and get lost, to have guilty pleasures and struggle to finish dense monstrosities.

If you're in a reading rut, make the next one you pick up a real page-turner. I used to get stuck because I felt obligated to finish every book I started, and because of that, I'd stop reading for months at a time. Similar to developing an exercise routine, diet plan, and a journaling practice, quitting is too easy when we have this all-or-nothing mindset. Now, I don't hesitate to drop a book and reread one of my favorite works of fiction like *Frankenstein* by Mary Shelley, *The Invisible Man* by Ralph Ellison, or *Ender's Game* by Orson Scott Card, to name a few.

If this is one of the only books you've read this year and you've never had a reading habit, please give it a try. I hope that this book had enough worthwhile ideas to get you to consider spending at least a few minutes a day with a book.

VIA NEGATIVA

The sculpture is already complete within the marble block, before I start my work. It is already there, I just have to chisel away the superfluous material.

—MICHELANGELO

This chapter has focused on adding or altering behaviors in ways that require new or different action. I have taken the time to talk about: exercise, hydration, sleep, diet, journaling, and reading habits.

This section is about removing, avoiding, or stopping behaviors. The title "via negativa" translates to "the negative way." It prioritizes a focus on reduction and removing to achieve a desired end. Michelangelo employed the negative way to create his famous sculpture *David*, and you can use it to sculpt a life that aligns with your vision.

I alluded to via negativa in the sections on diet, sleep, and journaling. You need to stop eating specific foods to have the health outcomes that you want. You should avoid blue light before bed to improve your sleep. Most importantly, you should identify what stupid behaviors you're engaged in and then work to disrupt and replace those habits.

As I've mentioned throughout this book, I spent an immense amount of my childhood playing video games. I do not regret it because I had a lot of fun, learned a lot, and built lasting friendships. However, as I headed to college, I knew that spending four hours or more a day playing video games would ruin my grades and take away from my college experience. I brought my desktop computer to college, but I uninstalled all the games I had been addicted to and replaced those multiple hours of gaming with time spent meeting new people, joining various organizations, and studying.

I was still down for playing hours of *Super Smash Bros* with my new friends, but I avoided becoming addicted to

League of Legends or a new Massive Multiplayer Online Role Playing Game (MMORPG). I would hear stories about my friends' roommates who lived in their dorm room, skipped class, and played *League* for fourteen hours a day. Many of those same friends later told me about how their roommate had not returned second semester because they had, unsurprisingly, failed their final exams. Not only did this lifestyle change prevent me from sharing their fate, but it has mostly persisted after college. I don't have the data, but I easily spend 1,000 less hours a year playing video games than I did in high school—the equivalent of twenty-five weeks of working full time.

If our lives are a complex network of habits, stimuli, and relationships, our role is to act as sculptors and cut away the excess to focus on our priorities. An understanding of the power of removing behavior that is either negative or a poor use of time is valuable for a leader. When you have so many responsibilities and demands on your time, removing behaviors is easier than adding new ones.

REFLECT: This would be a great opportunity for you to pull out your newly begun journal (even if it's just a few spare pages that you keep in a folder or the back of an old notebook) and reflect on the topic of via negativa.

A few prompts to consider:

- *What behaviors am I engaged in that I know are counter-productive to the future I want for myself?*

- *How might I replace those behaviors with more positive ones?*

- *How might I change my environment to facilitate those positive behaviors or deter the negative behaviors?*

- *How might I reward myself for changing my behavior?*

Via negativa may be one of the most powerful ideas in this entire book. As I mentioned earlier, we are often blind to these deeply entrenched habits because we've been practicing them for years or even decades. I am not encouraging you to become a monk and give up every form of recreation you enjoy. Keep playing those video games. Enjoy going out with your friends. Just be conscious and reflect on your behavior and see if there's anything you would be willing to sacrifice to create the future you want for yourself. Prioritization and time management are critical to the success of any leader. You have twenty-four hours in each day; the only way to create more time for yourself is to stop spending it elsewhere.

BE BORED

By meditating, we're learning to disengage ourselves from habitual clinging. ... We gradually learn to be more conscious and make better choices. We develop simplicity instead of complexity, open-mindedness instead of narrow-mindedness, flexibility rather than rigidity. We feel ourselves to be more available to others and to give more generously of ourselves.

—LAMA SURYA DAS, BUDDHA IS AS BUDDHA DOES: THE TEN ORIGINAL PRACTICES FOR ENLIGHTENED LIVING[90]

With your phone in your hand and your laptop in your bag, you can go days and even weeks without sitting in a calm boredom. You may feel bored after you watch the twentieth YouTube video or check Instagram or Twitter for the 33rd time of the day, but your mind will still be stimulated by the content. Escaping any awareness of your own thoughts is easy when you fill your head with the creations of others.

Meditation at its core is a practice of inaction. It is the choice to step away from the activities and concerns that stimulate your mind and seek peace by cultivating conscious awareness.

Rather than cite psychological research or quotes from household names who swear by meditation, I will remind you that this media-focused environment is a new invention.

---

90 ("A Quote From Buddha Is As Buddha Does" 2019)

The iPhone was invented in 2007. Fifty percent of Americans did not have household access to the internet until 2001. The television became a household item during the 1950s. The radio became popular in the 1920s.

Before these inventions, people spent much more time simply being present or at least bored. They might have been bored to be alone with their thoughts for hours a day, but maybe that's important.

If boredom is the great emotion of the TV generation, loneliness is the great emotion of the web generation. We lost the ability to be still, our capacity for idleness. They have lost the ability to be alone, their capacity for solitude.

And losing solitude, what have they lost? First, the propensity for introspection, that examination of the self that the Puritans, and the Romantics, and the modernists (and Socrates, for that matter) placed at the center of spiritual life—of wisdom, of conduct.

—WILLIAM DERESIEWICZ, "THE END OF SOLITUDE"[91]

Starting a practice of meditating is simple:

---

91   (Deresiewicz 2009)

- Find a quiet place where you can sit for ten minutes.
- Sit.
- Breathe in and out.

If you did that every day, you would develop a greater awareness of your mind than most people. It is that simple. After practicing for a few months, I go through precisely those three steps, although now I'll often meditate for even longer.

When I got started, I began by listening to a gratitude meditation that I found on YouTube called "Gratitude Meditation." If you want some initial guidance, that is a fine place to start. The gratitude practice gives you a direct reward for your practice by helping you generate positive feelings toward aspects of your life.

The only other advice that has been helpful during my practice has come from Tamara Levitt, who leads Content for Calm, a meditation app. When you are following your breath as part of your practice, your mind will wander, and you will become aware that you have begun to follow your thoughts rather than observe them as they pass by. Tamara, in one of her guided meditations, encouraged her listeners to view this awareness similar to how a weightlifter views a completed rep. Coming to awareness that your mind has wandered is the training and not something either good or bad.

After a couple weeks of daily meditation, I began to consciously experience the heightened awareness that it brought. While I find the practice to be an end in itself, I experienced joy in the subtle impact. I was walking through a hallway at my old job, heading to Starbucks to refill my reusable mug. As I was walking, I realized that my mind was running with thoughts about my next to-do, what I was going to eat for dinner, and how tired I was because I stayed up too late. In this moment of awareness, I consciously took a deep breath and was able to return to my breath and create a moment of peace. This simple experience brought me a great feeling of joy.

We all have a role in cultivating peace in our world, and meditation is a no-risk way toward that end.

STOP SCROLLING!

Did I mention that I've struggled to use my phone responsibly?

While I do know a few people who are able to use their phones as a tool without getting sucked into them for hours a day, most people don't have that experience. Different studies vary somewhat, but research shows that most cell phone users aged eighteen to thirty-four spend close to four hours a day on their cell phone.[92] If you include screen time spent

---

92 ("How Much Time Do People Spend On Their Mobile Phones In 2017?" 2017)

in front of a computer, particularly at work, I am sure that the average daily screen time is even more shocking.

Fortunately, phone companies are embedding tools to help their users better manage their usage. When my Android updated, being able to track my usage through the "Digital Wellbeing" setting did a lot to expand my consciousness about my behavior.

If you struggle with this problem, here are a few simple changes you can make:

- Actively track your daily usage through settings or an app on your phone or preferred device.

- Set an associated goal, e.g., "Use my phone for less than three hours per day for the next week." Reward yourself for achieving it.

- Remove the apps of platforms, i.e., Facebook, Twitter, etc., from your device and use the less enjoyable mobile versions.

- Turn off all push notifications—if people contact you through these platforms, simply let them know that you've changed your settings.

- Schedule specific times and a limited amount of time to spend using these apps.

- Consciously take one day off from using social media, or even any device, per week.

Sticking to the status quo of compulsive usage is much easier. But, if your usage has approached 4+ hours a day, your phone habits are not a good use of your time. As we've discussed throughout this chapter, the consistent practice of a habit can significantly impact your life and skill sets.

My friend Vita's app, deprocrastination.co, is a series of tools to help people to change their digital habits. He created this tool to help more people overcome their addiction and desire to procrastinate. His reframe about what you could do with the extra time is just as powerful:

$1.01^{365}=37.78$

If you got 1 percent better at a skill every day, you would be 37.78 times better by the end of the year.

If all that meant was you needed to spend 1 percent of your day practicing a skill—like drawing, writing, or learning a language—you would only need to spend fourteen minutes and twenty-four seconds of your time to achieve these results.[93]

Even if you only got a tenth of a percent (1.001) better at a skill by practicing for fourteen minutes a day, you would still be 44 percent better if you practiced every day for a year.

If you could replace thirty minutes of mindless scrolling with two intentional sessions of working on your skill stack or exploring a hobby, you could change the trajectory of your life.

ACTION:

- *If you have a usage tracker on your preferred device, go look through your daily usage.*

- *If you do not have one, search for an app that will enable you to track this information.*

- *Turn off your push notifications.*

- *Delete any apps that you know are not a good use of your time and energy.*

---

93 (Benes 2018)

- *Write a reflection on your screen time. How it is valuable to you? How it is harmful to you?*

My hope with this section is not to shame anyone for their usage. Ultimately, if you do not think your time could be better spent elsewhere or you have no problem with your usage, feel free to continue on as usual.

AMISH HACKERS

Kevin Kelly, technologist and essayist of "1,000 True Fans," was the first person to reframe technology use for me. Here is an excerpt from another essay he wrote called *Amish Hackers:*

> The Amish are steadily adopting technology — at their pace. They are slow geeks. As one Amish man told Howard Rheingold, 'We don't want to stop progress, we just want to slow it down.' But their manner of slow adoption is instructive.
>
> 1) They are selective. They know how to say 'no' and are not afraid to refuse new things. They ban more than they adopt.
>
> 2) They evaluate new things by experience instead of by theory. They let the early

adopters get their jollies by pioneering new stuff under watchful eyes.

3) They have criteria by which to select choices: technologies must enhance family and community and distance themselves from the outside world.

4) The choices are not individual, but communal. The community shapes and enforces technological direction.

Before reading Kelly's essay, I was completely uneducated about the technological practices of the Amish. He opens his essay with this sentence: "The Amish have the undeserved reputation of being luddites, of people who refuse to employ new technology."[94] I now understand this perception of the Amish to be totally inaccurate.

In point three in the above quote, Kelly succinctly articulates the ethics of the Amish people's decision to adopt or reject a new technology. This concept in itself was foreign to me. For most Americans, including myself, the primary criteria of deciding to adopt a technology seem to be as follows:

---

94 (Kelly 2009)

- Has it been marketed to me?
- Are others adopting it?
- Can I afford it?

I bring this up to introduce the concept of developing an ethic around technology. It has changed dramatically throughout my lifetime and it seems unlikely that new widgets and tools will cease to be marketed to us. If we're going to decide to avoid adoption and remove technologies from our lives, we're going to need to develop individual ethics to guide our usage.

REFLECT: How has technology changed your life for the best? How has technology made your life worse? Are there any technologies you have consciously decided to avoid? As always, I recommend a written reflection on these points, but even more so, I suggest engaging your friends and family in a discussion on this topic.

As we saw through my own struggle in chapter four, your habits are critical to your success as a leader. If you can work to develop habits aligned with your vision for yourself, you will experience a powerful transformation. Not only will you progress in the ways that your habits help you to, but you will recognize that you are capable of more than you might imagine.

CONCLUSION

———

Being imaginative and dreaming is absolutely important.
Don't let anybody tell you otherwise and don't let consider-
ations of "the practical" mute or dull your ability to dream.

—PAUL J. BURGETT, MUSICIAN, COMMUNITY LEADER[95]

This book is full of "the practical." Pragmatic advice, powerful frameworks, and calls to action to devote yourself to
solving critical problems. I hope you will use these tools to
lead in whatever capacity you wish to—whether that means
creating the next revolutionary company, leading an organization you're part of, or collaborating with your neighbors
to clean up your street and plant flower beds.

———

95   (University of Rochester 2013)

But I fully agree with the advice of my late mentor Paul J. Burgett above. We need people who imagine, dream, and inspire. If anything I wrote in this book made you want to abandon a dream you have, don't let it. Instead, I hope you will use this moment of doubt to push yourself to pursue your dreams.

Dean Burgett not only challenged people to continue to dream and imagine but also, through his example, to reconsider their conventional ideas of success. Year after year, many students would arrive at the college with the belief that the only way to be successful was to become a big fish in a big pond. They hoped their hard work would earn them a ticket to whichever elite community they aspired to join.

He challenged this idea by embodying a different paradigm of success. Instead of taking his talents elsewhere in the pursuit of amassing as much money and power as possible, he dedicated his energy and creativity to the university and the Rochester community. When you heard his booming voice share anecdotes about the support he had provided to various students and people throughout the community, over his decades of service, you could not help but reconsider your priorities. His life was clearly filled with meaning and his contributions to his community were invaluable. He was a role model for a lifestyle that receives a tragically small amount of consideration.

I mention his example to emphasize the importance of your values, goals, and the actions you choose to take. You are a leader. You are a role model. The decisions you make and how you choose to spend your time matter.

Leadership is not about the power you have in a hierarchy. It's about acknowledging a different kind of power—leadership is about your understanding of how your actions and decisions will influence the lives of others. Leadership is about your ability to envision a future that is different from today and collaborate with others to turn it into a reality. Leadership is about your mindset and how you can leverage your knowledge and skill sets to solve problems and influence others to join you.

Leadership is about your relationship with the future.

Please consider and reflect on:

- The principles of leadership, as we discussed in chapter three

- How you can create habits, learn from my mistakes, and avoid burnout, as we discussed in chapters four and nine

- The implications of acknowledging complexity and the necessity of feedback and accountability for leaders, as we discussed in chapter five

- The power of building and maintaining close partnerships, as we discussed in chapters six and seven

- Power laws and how they relate to your day-to-day experience in the world, as we discussed in chapter seven

- The need for a movement toward definite optimism (and the virtues of pessimism), as we discussed in chapter seven

- Your skill stack and how you can develop habits that will help you to expand your opportunities and influence, as we discussed in chapters seven and nine

I hope to look back on the decision to write this book as a turning point in my career as a leader. Likewise, I hope that's how you will see your decision to read this book. If you want to improve your leadership abilities, you should make space to reflect on your values and the frameworks we've explored throughout this book. And, most importantly, apply that new understanding to realize your vision for the future. Unfortunately, reading through the pages without any action or deeper reflection is unlikely to impact your life in any significant way.

While this part of our journey together has come to an end, I hope that this moment marks the beginning of a greater adventure together. It's going to be challenging, but we can overcome the obstacles that we face. We will get stronger and gain experience that will change us in ways we cannot anticipate.

If the introduction was a tap on your shoulder telling you it's time to be awesome, the conclusion is a high-five telling you that it's time to set goals, develop habits, and accept responsibility.

I believe in our ability to lead others into a more prosperous and meaningful future. Let's get to it.

ACTION: Send me an email at grantdever@gmail.com with the subject "Finished Your Book."

ACKNOWLEDGEMENTS

———

Writing a book has been even more difficult than I had expected. I would not have decided to begin this venture, let alone completed it, without the support of many people throughout my life.

I would like to thank my Mom for being my role model. Throughout my life she has been my local leader and taught me the importance of leading by example. Her hardwork and compassion help me to recognize that there's still so much more I can learn.

I would like to thank my Dad for cultivating my curiosity and passion for reading. Without his encouragement, I do not know that I would have spent as much time reading as I have.

Likewise, I am grateful for your support, advice and for you always pushing me to be rigorous when I make life decisions.

I would like to thank my step mom DiDi for her unconditional support and all of the hard work she put in to ensure I had a wonderful upbringing. Furthermore, without her, I would have eaten pizza or cereal for many more meals. Coming home from my adventures is not only heartwarming but delicious.

I would like to thank my brother Clark for being my first mentor and providing me with advice and encouragement to pursue most of the adventures described in this book. He is now leading by example in so many aspects of his life. I am incredibly proud of his achievements and the quality of his and Kelly's family. Hi Maverick and Minerva, I hope this book is still interesting when it's age appropriate.

I would like to thank Nick Sparacino for being my day one friend and giving me an early insight into the benefits of multi-decade friendships. Shoutout to Mac Liu, Jake Barkin, Joey Stephens, Taylor Road Gang, my Homies, and The Boys who have all supported me on this journey and will all join Slick in being multi-decade friends.

I would like to thank Melissa Holloway, Antoinette Esce, Greg Corrado, and Emma Pollock for their mentorship and for allowing me to feature them throughout this text in various ways. Each of you inspire me with your work ethic and help me to grow by challenging my thinking and assumptions.

I would like to thank my team at iZone for all that they taught me and in recognition of our future collaborations: Barbara J. Burger, Mary Ann Mavrinac, Julia Maddox, Deniz Cengiz, Anush Mehrabyan, Vlad Cazacu, Zoe Tzetzis, Ewin Joseph, James Pike, Dewey Bazirake, Maria Hackett, Michael Keane, Allie Fredrickson, Shannon Lue Chee Lip, Maggie Peng (Thanks for the graphics!), Ellen Yuetong, Victoria Ter-Ovanesyan, and Mike Arinarkin.

I would like to specially recognize Julia Maddox, my first full-time boss and co-founder. Thank you for all that you taught me throughout our time working together at iZone. Your leadership at iZone has been critical to its success and I am impressed by what your leadership has been able to accomplish in such a short time. Thank you for your continued support and I am excited for our next collaboration.

I would like to thank the Metzler family for their generous support throughout this process. You have a lovely family and I greatly appreciate your kindness. Luke has inspired me to shoot for the stars through his example. I could not be more proud of Luke's successes as a performer and writer, or optimistic about his trajectory.

I would like to thank the Barkin family for their love and kindness throughout this process and my life. You all have taught me so much and I am grateful for my relationships with all of you.

I would like to thank Nomi Bergman for her mentorship and generous support throughout this process. I am so grateful to have you as a role model and mentor. Your commitment to Rochester and WNY inspire me to never forget the communities that have given me so much.

I would like to thank Judy and Paul Linehan for their generous support throughout this process and my entire life. You both have continually enabled me to access so many opportunities and it has made all the difference. I cannot imagine how different my life would be without my relationship with both of you and I am so grateful and inspired by your generosity.

I would like to thank everyone at New Degree Press for their support every step of the way. Brian Bies for all of his hard work to keep me on deadline. Cortni Merritt for her contributions and willingness to brainstorm as my Developmental Editor. Heather Gomez for her feedback and insights as my Marketing Editor. Catriona Kendall for her amazing copy-editing which helped me to publish a polished book that y'all are proud to be recognized in.

I would like to thank Eric Koester for convincing me that I could write a book and his support throughout the process. Without his insights and his success in convincing my dear friend Vlad Cazacu to lead by example, I am certain that I never would have started this journey. Eric inspires me to figure out how I can effectively scale my impact on the world.

I would like to thank Julianne McAdams for her phenomenal work editing drafts of my book. This book would not have been ready for copy-editing without her dedication and talent. Julianne has always inspired me to become a better writer and I am so grateful for our friendship. I look forward to future adventures and collaborations. I sincerely hope this is just the beginning.

I would like to thank David Stark and Matt Skurnick (Tel Aviv, Israel), Georgi Hristozov (Sofia, Bulgaria), the Käbisch Family (Grossauheim, Germany), and the Liu Family (China) for hosting me as I worked on this book while traveling abroad. Without their generosity and warmth, I would not have been able to continue my travels.

I would like to thank everyone who supported my campaign in numerous ways: pre-ordering copies of the book, providing feedback on drafts, giving input the cover, and sending messages of support. There are so many more people that I could recognize and I will be sure to do that in-person and perhaps on my blog!

APPENDIX

———

INTRODUCTION

"A Quote From The Unbearable Lightness Of Being". 2019. *Goodreads.Com.* https://www.goodreads.com/quotes/198627-culture-is-perishing-in-overproduction-in-an-avalanche-of-words.

CT Staff. 2019. "Campus Times Endorses Grant Dever And Melissa Holloway For SA President And Vice President - Campus Times". *Campus Times.* http://www.campustimes.org/2015/04/05/campus-times-endorses-grant-dever-and-melissa-holloway-for-sa-president-and-vice-president/.

CHAPTER 1: GRANTMAN ORIGINS

CHAPTER 2: DEFINING LEADERSHIP

"Ashoka U Exchange 2019: Beyond Boundaries & Borders - The Association For The Advancement Of Sustainability In Higher Education". 2019. *The Association For The Advancement Of Sustainability In Higher Education.* https://www.aashe.org/calendar/ashoka-u-exchange-2019-beyond-boundaries-borders/.

Austin, Kathy. 2019. "A Quote By Kathy Austin". *Goodreads.Com.* https://www.goodreads.com/quotes/622625-managers-light-a-fire-under-people-leaders-light-a-fire.

"A Quote By Harriet Tubman". 2019. *Goodreads.*
Com. https://www.goodreads.com/
quotes/5935-every-great-dream-begins-with-a-dreamer-always-remember-you.

"A Quote From Management". 2019. *Goodreads.*
Com. https://www.goodreads.com/
quotes/656219-leadership-is-not-magnetic-personality-that-can-just-as-well.

"Martin Luther King, Jr. Quotes". 2019. *Brainyquote.* https://www.brainyquote.
com/quotes/martin_luther_king_jr_166528.

CHAPTER 3: PRINCIPLES OF LEADERSHIP

Gallup, Inc. 2019. "The No. 1 Employee Benefit That No One's Talking About".
Gallup.Com. https://www.gallup.com/workplace/232955/no-employee-bene-
fit-no-one-talking.aspx.

Gallup, Inc. 2019. "Confidence In Institutions". *Gallup.Com.* https://news.
gallup.com/poll/1597/confidence-institutions.aspx.

Kouzes, James M., and Barry Z. Posner. 2010. *The Truth About Leadership: The
No-Fads, Heart-Of-The-Matter Facts You Need To Know.* Ebook. 1st ed. San
Francisco: Jossey-Bass.

Kowitt, Beth. 2015. "Whole Foods' John Mackey: The Conscious Capitalist".
Fortune. https://fortune.com/2015/08/20/whole-foods-john-mackey/.

Mackey, John. 2009. "The Whole Foods Alternative To Obamacare". *WSJ.*
https://www.wsj.com/articles/SB10001424052970204251404574342170072865070.

Schumacher, Jon. 2019. "How Whole Foods CEO John Mackey Is Leading A
Revolution In Health And Business". *Entrepreneur.* https://www.entrepreneur.
com/article/325128.

CHAPTER 4: REALITIES OF LEADERSHIP

"Mike Tyson Quotes". 2019. *Brainyquote.* https://www.brainyquote.com/quotes/
mike_tyson_382439.

Richards, Gareth, and Andrew Smith. 2015. "Caffeine Consumption And
Self-Assessed Stress, Anxiety, And Depression In Secondary School Children".
Journal Of Psychopharmacology 29 (12): 1236-1247. doi:10.1177/0269881115612404.

van Mierlo, Trevor. 2014. "The 1% Rule In Four Digital Health Social Networks: An Observational Study". *Journal Of Medical Internet Research* 16 (2): e33. doi:10.2196/jmir.2966.

CHAPTER 5: ALL MODELS ARE WRONG, SOME ARE USEFUL

"A Quote From Flecks Of Gold On A Path Of Stone". 2019. *Goodreads.Com*. https://www.goodreads.com/ quotes/6898089-to-be-careless-in-making-decisions-is-to-naively-believe.

Clarey, Christopher. 2014. "Olympians Use Imagery As Mental Training". *Nytimes.Com*. https://www.nytimes.com/2014/02/23/sports/olympics/olympi-ans-use-imagery-as-mental-training.html.

Fernholz, Tim. 2019. "Elon Musk Is Building A Fleet Of Reusable Rockets". *Quartz*. https://qz.com/1651552/ elon-musks-falcon-heavy-leads-a-fleet-of-reusable-rockets/.

Freiburger, Marianne. 2014. "Chaos On The Billiard Table". *Plus.Maths.Org*. https://plus.maths.org/content/chaos-billiard-table.

"Friedrich Nietzsche Quotes". 2019. *Brainyquote*. https://www.brainyquote.com/ quotes/friedrich_nietzsche_103819.

Lee, Jae Seung. 2019. "Minimum Wage In The Era Of Automation". *The Economics Review At NYU*. https://theeconreview.com/2019/04/22/ minimum-wage-in-the-era-of-automation/.

Öhman, Arne, and Susan Mineka. 2003. "The Malicious Serpent". *Current Directions In Psychological Science* 12 (1): 5-9. doi:10.1111/1467-8721.01211.

Ramnerö, Jonas, and Niklas Törneke. 2014. "On Having A Goal: Goals As Representations Or Behavior". *The Psychological Record* 65 (1): 89-99. doi:10.1007/ s40732-014-0093-0.

Rozin, Paul, and Edward B. Royzman. 2001. "Negativity Bias, Negativity Dominance, And Contagion". *Personality And Social Psychology Review* 5 (4): 296-320. doi:10.1207/s15327957pspr0504_2

CHAPTER 6: IZONE MAFIA

"iZone". 2019. *iZone At University Of Rochester.* https://izone.lib.rochester.edu/.'

"Paypal Mafia | Wikipedia". 2019. *Wikipedia.* https://www.wikipedia.com/en/PayPal_Mafia.

Ravikant, Naval. 2019. "Play Long-Term Games With Long-Term People". *Naval.* https://nav.al/long-term.

CHAPTER 7: THE POWER LAW OF YOU

"A Quote By Henry Ford". 2019. *Goodreads.Com.* https://www.goodreads.com/quotes/978-whether-you-think-you-can-or-you-think-you-can-t--you-re.

BBC Radio. 2017. *If You're A Kanye West Fan You're A Fan Of Yourself.* Video. https://www.youtube.com/watch?v=7eSFDuX2bMQ.

Cadwalladr, Carole. 2014. "Wikipedia's Jimmy Wales: 'It's True, I'm Not A Billionaire. So?' – Interview". *The Guardian.* https://www.theguardian.com/technology/2014/feb/07/jimmy-wales-wikipedia-interview.

Changes In U.S. Family Finances From 2013 To 2016: Evidence From The Survey Of Consumer Finances. 2017. Ebook. Board of Governors of the Federal Reserve System. https://www.federalreserve.gov/publications/files/scf17.pdf.

Covey, Stephen. 2019. "Habit 1". *Franklincovey.Com.* https://www.franklincovey.com/the-7-habits/habit-1.html.

Cowen, Tyler, and Daniel Kahneman. 2018. "My Conversation With Daniel Kahneman - Marginal REVOLUTION". *Marginal REVOLUTION.* https://marginalrevolution.com/marginalrevolution/2018/12/conversation-daniel-kahneman.html.

"Friedrich Nietzsche Quote". 2019. *A-Z Quotes.* https://www.azquotes.com/quote/1231021.

"Instagram Follower Rates 2018 | Mention.Com". 2018. *Mention.Com.* https://mention.com/en/reports/instagram/followers/#2.

Kelly, Kevin. 2016. "The Technium: 1,000 True Fans". *Kk.Org.* https://kk.org/thetechnium/1000-true-fans/.

Kids See Ghosts. *Reborn.* 2018. Album. Jackson Hole: GOOD Music; Def Jam.

"Kim Kardashian West (@Kimkardashian) • Instagram Photos And Videos".
2019. *Instagram.Com*. https://www.instagram.com/kimkardashian/?hl=en.

MacCarthy, Ryan. 2016. "The Average Twitter User Now Has 707 Followers -
Science Of Social Sales". *Science Of Social Sales*. https://kickfactory.com/blog/
average-twitter-followers-updated-2016/.

Murphy, David. 2014. "44 Percent Of Twitter Accounts
Have Never Tweeted". *PCMAG*. https://www.pcmag.com/
news/322611/44-percent-of-twitter-accounts-have-never-tweeted.

Parry, Steve. 2008. "BBC SPORT | Olympics Blog". *Bbc.Co.Uk*. https://www.bbc.
co.uk/blogs/olympics/2008/08/can_anyone_spoil_phelps_pool_p.html.

Rosenberg, Eric. 2018. "How Google Makes Money (GOOG)". *Investopedia*.
https://www.investopedia.com/articles/investing/020515/business-google.asp.

"Search Engine Market Share". 2017. *Netmarketshare.Com*. https://netmarket-
share.com/search-engine-market-share.aspx.

Sivers, Derek. 2019. "How To Get Rich | Derek Sivers". *Sivers.Org*. https://sivers.org/d1r.

Terdiman, Daniel. 2013. "Elon Musk At SXSW: 'I'd Like To Die On
Mars, Just Not On Impact'". *CNET*. https://www.cnet.com/news/
elon-musk-at-sxsw-id-like-to-die-on-mars-just-not-on-impact/.

Thiel, Peter, and Blake Masters. 2014. *Zero To One: Notes On Startups, Or How
To Build The Future*. Ebook. New York City: Currency.

Webb, Kevin. 2018. "'Fortnite' Streamer Tyler 'Ninja' Blevins Says He Once
Received A $40,000 Donation While Playing The Game". *Business Insider
Deutschland*. https://www.businessinsider.de/fortnite-streamer-tyler-ninja-
blevins-received-40000-donation-playing-game-2018-9?r=US&IR=T.

West, Kanye, and Ty Dolla $ign. 2016. *Real Friends*. Album. GOOD; Def Jam.

"Ye (@Kanyewest) On Twitter". 2019. *Twitter.Com*. https://twitter.com/kanyewest.

Zadek, Bob. 2018. "Jonathan Haidt On *The Coddling Of The American
Mind*". *Medium*. https://medium.com/@rzadek/trigger-warning-jonathan-
haidt-on-the-coddling-of-the-american-mind-6c71014d28b6.

CHAPTER 8: AMATEUR ECONOMICS

Drug Decriminalization In Portugal: A Health-Centered Approach. 2015. Ebook. New York City: Drug Policy Alliance.

Ingraham, Chris. 2015. "The EU Country Where Drugs Are Decriminalised – And Hardly Anyone Dies Of An Overdose". *The Independent.* https://www.independent.co.uk/news/world/europe/portugal-decriminalised-drugs-14-years-ago-and-now-hardly-anyone-dies-from-overdosing-10301780.html.

"Vital Statistics Rapid Release - Provisional Drug Overdose Data". 2018. *Cdc. Gov.* https://www.cdc.gov/nchs/nvss/vsrr/drug-overdose-data.htm.

CHAPTER 9: 80/20 HABITS OF HIGHLY EFFECTIVE LEADERS

"A Quote From A Dance With Dragons". 2019. *Goodreads.Com.* https://www.goodreads.com/quotes/408441-a-reader-lives-a-thousand-lives-before-he-dies-said

"A Quote From Buddha Is As Buddha Does". 2019. *Goodreads.Com.* https://www.goodreads.com/quotes/678400-by-meditating-we-re-learning-to-disengage-ourselves-from-habitual-clinging.

Benes, Vita. 2019. "Twitter". *Twitter.com.* https://twitter.com/vitabenes/status/1166797899713449984.

Deresiewicz, William. 2009. "The End Of Solitude By William Deresiewicz". *Hermitary.Com.* https://www.hermitary.com/solitude/deresiewicz.html.

Ferriss, Tim, and Jim Collins. 2019. "Jim Collins — A Rare Interview With A Reclusive Polymath (#361)". *The Blog Of Author Tim Ferriss.* https://tim.blog/2019/02/18/jim-collins/.

Fox, Justin, and Charles Duhigg. 2012. "Habits: Why We Do What We Do". *Harvard Business Review.* https://hbr.org/2012/06/habits-why-we-do-what-we-do.

Heijnen, Saskia, Bernhard Hommel, Armin Kibele, and Lorenza S. Colzato. 2016. "Neuromodulation Of Aerobic Exercise—A Review". *Frontiers In Psychology* 6. doi:10.3389/fpsyg.2015.01890.

"How Much Time Do People Spend On Their Mobile Phones In 2017?". 2017. *Hackernoon.Com.* https://hackernoon.com/how-much-time-do-people-spend-on-their-mobile-phones-in-2017-e5f90a0b10a6.

Krause, Adam J., Eti Ben Simon, Bryce A. Mander, Stephanie M. Greer, Jared M. Saletin, Andrea N. Goldstein-Piekarski, and Matthew P. Walker. 2017. "The Sleep-Deprived Human Brain". *Nature Reviews Neuroscience* 18 (7): 404-418. doi:10.1038/nrn.2017.55.

"Mortality In The United States, 2017". 2018. *Cdc.Gov.* https://www.cdc.gov/nchs/products/databriefs/db328.htm.

Myers, Jonathan. 2003. "Exercise And Cardiovascular Health". *Circulation* 107 (1). doi:10.1161/01.cir.0000048890.59383.8d.

Patsalos, Olivia C., and Volker Thoma. 2019. "Water Supplementation After Dehydration Improves Judgment And Decision-Making Performance". *Psychological Research.* doi:10.1007/s00426-018-1136-y.

Perrin, Andrew. 2016. "Majority Of Americans Are Still Reading Print Books". *Pew Research Center: Internet, Science & Tech.* https://www.pewinternet. org/2016/09/01/book-reading-2016/.

"Research Progress About The Effect And Prevention Of Blue Light On Eyes". 2018. *International Journal Of Ophthalmology.* doi:10.18240/ijo.2018.12.20.

Saul, Heather. 2016. "Why Mark Zuckerberg Wears The Same Clothes To Work Everyday". *The Independent.* https://www.independent.co.uk/news/people/why-mark-zuckerberg-wears-the-same-clothes-to-work-everyday-a6834161.html.

Stenvers, Dirk Jan, Rick van Dorp, Ewout Foppen, Jorge Mendoza, Anne-Loes Opperhuizen, Eric Fliers, Peter H. Bisschop, Johanna H. Meijer, Andries Kalsbeek, and Tom Deboer. 2016. "Dim Light At Night Disturbs The Daily Sleep-Wake Cycle In The Rat". *Scientific Reports* 6 (1). doi:10.1038/srep35662.

Tomporowski, Phillip D., Catherine L. Davis, Patricia H. Miller, and Jack A. Naglieri. 2007. "Exercise And Children'S Intelligence, Cognition, And Academic Achievement". *Educational Psychology Review* 20 (2): 111-131. doi:10.1007/s10648-007-9057-0.

Wilhelmi de Toledo, Françoise, Franziska Grundler, Audrey Bergouignan, Stefan Drinda, and Andreas Michalsen. 2019. "Safety, Health Improvement And Well-Being During A 4 To 21-Day Fasting Period In An Observational Study Including 1422 Subjects". *PLOS ONE* 14 (1): e0209353. doi:10.1371/journal.pone.0209353.

Yates, Jon. 2003. "Chicago Tribune - Zoos On Mission To Find Why Polar Bears Lost In Pace". *Chicagotribune.com.* https://www.chicagotribune.com/news/ct-xpm-2003-11-30-0311300462-story.html..

Benes, Vita. 2018. "How To Transform Yourself Into Your Ideal". *Vitabenes. com*. http://vitabenes.com/how-to-transform-yourself-into-your-ideal.

CONCLUSION

University of Rochester. 2013. *Paul Burgett: "The Fiery Furnace"*. Video. https://www.youtube.com/watch?v=br5bGe3HyX0.

Made in the USA
Coppell, TX
11 May 2021

55477497R00131